Unity through Community Service Activities

Unity through Community Service Activities

Strategies to Bridge Ethnic and Cultural Divides

AUGUST JOHN HOFFMAN,
NORMA ESPINOSA PARKER,
EDUARDO SANCHEZ
and JULIE WALLACH

McFarland & Company, Inc., Publishers
Jefferson, North Carolina, and London

The authors would like to thank the California State University Northridge Center for Innovative and Educational Opportunities (CIELO) for the numerous grants in making this community service work to Compton College possible. CIELO support, with the help of Merri Whitelock and Donna Brooks, have contributed to improving the lives, communities and careers of hundreds of students.

LIBRARY OF CONGRESS CATALOGUING-IN-PUBLICATION DATA

Unity through community service activities : strategies to bridge ethnic and cultural divides / August John Hoffman ... [et al.].
p.   cm.
Includes bibliographical references and index.

ISBN 978-0-7864-4108-2
softcover : 50# alkaline paper ∞

1. Social work education.   I. Hoffman, August John.
HV11.U617   2009   361.2'5 — dc22   2009001524

British Library cataloguing data are available

Cover photographs ©2009 Photodisc

Manufactured in the United States of America

McFarland & Company, Inc., Publishers
Box 611, Jefferson, North Carolina 28640
www.mcfarlandpub.com

Table of Contents

Introduction

Why Write a Book about Community Service Work?

Many of my colleagues have asked just that question. Why write a book about activities performed within a community by various groups of people? What does community service work have to do with learning and people's behaviors today? The best possible answer to this important question is to try to first imagine a city, community or society that lacks the resources or impetus to organize groups of individuals in improving the areas where they live. Imagine an "interpersonally sterile" environment where all people were essentially alienated from each other and their time was spent individually, consumed by some form of technological service (i.e., video games, cell phones, etc.). The result would be a community without a sense of a group identity, one that lacks in potential, community pride and aptitude. The result would also be a self-absorbed group of individuals who lack the capacity to engage and prosocially respond with each other.

What Is Community Service Work?

Community service work is just that — work that is conducted by the community members for the community members. It is about organizing groups of individuals to help each other and their community. Community service work also is highly advantageous in that it brings people together and helps provide a common link for each person. Community service work operates on a collective self-efficacy principle — the more we work together, the more we can accomplish together. One key term that we will continually revisit throughout this book is that of *interdependency* — the awareness of the need to be needed and to feel connected to a larger group. This is why our communities today need community service activities, perhaps more than ever, to allow us to work together and collectively and achieve meaning and purpose in the process.

Community service work is rapidly becoming a key component in our society that defines how individuals relate and interact with each other, and more importantly, how individuals define and achieve meaning within their lives. Community service work refers to any activity that combines the efforts of a group that is designed to improve some aspect of the community. Perhaps more important than even the end product of community service work is the process itself — groups of diverse individuals realizing their potential is only achieved through cooperation with others. This is a most powerful dynamic that *can* move mountains.

Group efforts in cleaning up a park or cleaning a beach of litter, civic activities that improve the aesthetic environment such as planting trees in an urban environment, and improving a community center by planting flowers and removing graffiti are all positive examples of community service work. In this text we look at the topics of community service work and the potentially negative alternatives of a multiethnic society that cannot (or refuses to) integrate and assimilate with each other.

At best, a lack of understanding of individuals from diverse ethnic backgrounds limits our own personal growth and understanding of others that prevents us from effective interaction with other people in our environment who may come from different cultural backgrounds. At the very worst, a limited understanding of human diversity can create hostile environments that may quickly become polarized and may even lead to conflict and violence. The primary scope and purpose of this text is in describing how community service learning principles can facilitate interethnic group development and reduce ethnic conflict. We maintain that communities and educational institutions need to develop more community service programs that allow individuals from different ethnic groups to better interact and understand each other.

When groups of individuals engage in aggression and hostility simply because of a perceived difference in ethnicity or culture, we as a community need to intervene and educate as a means to reduce the violence. What is especially disturbing today is that these crimes involving ethnocentrism and ethnic violence are occurring in younger populations. What is perhaps even more disturbing is that the majority of these ethnic hate crimes could have been prevented with simple planning and intervention skills.

In a disturbing trend, *The Daily News* (Friday, 6/8/07) reported that more youths were taking part in hate crimes, and that the number of hate crimes involving juveniles rose to 233 and accounted for 43 percent of all suspects involved in similar crimes, up 32 percent in 2005. Additionally, gang behavior has been identified as a key component and contributor to hate crimes, where one in five (20 percent) hate crimes is committed by gang members. Among African Americans as victims, the number of cases rose slightly, from 230 to 237 in 2006 (Los Angeles County Human Relations Commission). In a more recent incident, *The Daily News* (Thursday, 10/11/07) reported three African American students were involved in an altercation with a Caucasian security guard over the students allegedly not picking up litter at Knight High School, a high school located in Palmdale, California. The city of Palmdale is rapidly becoming ethnically diverse, where now Latinos outnumber Caucasian students 47 percent to 39 percent, with the African American population estimated at approximately 17 percent (U.S. Census data, 2006). This recent increase in the demographic changes of Palmdale underscores the importance and need for communities facing increases in ethnic diversity to adapt programs and educational seminars that facilitate ethnic integration and assimilation.

This incident followed the racial conflict in Jena, Louisiana, where six African American teenagers were charged with assault on a Caucasian classmate. The incident was prompted by several nooses being hung from a tree at Jena High School, an action that was designed to intimidate and taunt African American students at the high school. More recently, the Los Angeles City Council voted 11 to 0 in support of a "symbolic moratorium" in banning the use of the "N-word" (*Los Angeles Daily News*, Saturday, November 10, 2007). Unfortunately, there are several more examples of racially motivated aggressive activities throughout our country. It is critical that we respond proactively in trying to develop mechanisms that may defuse these potentially destructive and violent episodes from reoccurring. The information contained in this book is specifically designed to help bring people from diverse backgrounds together to work cooperatively with each other within our community.

Humans have historically demonstrated skills and aptitudes in their ability to work cooperatively with each other as a means of improving their overall quality of living. Throughout our evolutionary and developmental history, different groups of individuals combined and shared resources to help each other in times of need. This unique capacity to work interactively and reciprocally with each other is very similar to the benefits of community service work. Attitudes and relationships improve significantly when ethnically diverse groups work cooperatively together for a common goal. In this sense, then, we must understand that humans can certainly do more than develop limited and narrow-minded "tolerance" for one another. We can value and appreciate each other (as well as celebrating our differences) and grow from our experiences and make rational proactive decisions that can improve the quality of life for all persons via the concept of belonging and interdependency (Smith, Spillane, & Annus, 2006).

Furthermore, we can do significantly more than simply tolerate each other; we can *thrive* by understanding how our cultural differences can provide positive meaning to human interaction. There were several reasons why we began writing this text, but our primary goal was to identify the various techniques used in community service work to reduce ethnic hostility and to promote communication and positive interaction among different ethnic groups within our community. All persons representing all ethnic groups need to become proactive in their approach to discovering methods in improving their personal and professional relationships with each other.

There are many things that we as a unified group can do to improve our relationships with each other. Simply "tolerating" each other implies that different ethnic groups inherently are in conflict with each other, a premise that we hope to illustrate as being patently false. We *can* understand each other and grow to learn, appreciate and value diversity within the community, but first people must be shown the process and methodology in achieving these important goals.

There are many reasons why interethnic group relationships are experiencing racial conflict and deteriorating today. We have constructed each chapter in this book to explore different ways and methods to approach this problem. Chapter 1 first discusses the dynamic relationship between community service learning, cooperative groups and how group development can establish a key element in our society: interdependency. The development of groups can provide individuals with the impetus and momentum to achieve a broad range of goals. However, groups by themselves do not naturally become dynamic and positive forces. Groups must first tap into each individual member's talents and skills and combine them with other group members' potential. In our empirical work we hope to show how ethnically diverse groups may work towards common goals and significantly improve their relationships with each other. It is precisely within the process of achieving our goals that we learn to appreciate the diversity of each group member. We will also explore how groups may be constructed for maximum development and how individuals have evolved with the need for mentoring skills as a key element to effective group participation.

Chapter 2 addresses our evolutionary history and how groups played a critical role relative to our survival. The more that we can understand how our behaviors were adaptive during our evolutionary history, the better we can understand our behavior today in group dynamics and interethnic group participation. Additionally, we explore how important communication and decision-making processes are established within groups.

Chapter 3 is concernted with how roles are developed once groups have been assigned, and how the hierarchy within members of the group influences group interaction. This chapter is important relative to community work principles, as individuals within groups tend to form roles among each group member.

Chapter 4 explores the role of cooperative learning in group development and community service projects. Perhaps more than ever within our community, individuals need the opportunity to "give back" or to contribute to the community as a means of discovering their place and role within the community itself. More importantly, in our empirical research we have discovered that ethnically diverse groups can actually improve their relationships (i.e., reduce in ethnocentrism) with each other when they engage in cooperative group assignments.

Chapter 5 takes up the role of interdependency as a key factor in helping people work cooperatively together, and without it, how human behavior can become counterproductive and even destructive.

Chapter 6 considers how community service work improves communication skills and reduces ethnocentrism in the student population.

A key element to Chapter 7 addresses the relationship between collectivistic and individualistic characteristics with community service learning principles and how these characteristics influence group development. All too often in our society today individuals remain highly competitive and do not view others within the group as a resource to work cooperatively in achieving goals. The collectivistic philosophy is critical to successful group development and community service work.

Chapter 8 discusses how prejudice and discrimination influence group decisions and how cooperative group work can foster the key element of interdependency. Interdependency refers to the need to contribute to the group as well as the awareness of what unique skills an individual may possess to contribute to the group as a means of maintaining integrity.

If we assume that one basis of racism is a separatist philosophy and sense of feeling inherently different (i.e., superior) than others, then group work that is designed to achieve interdependency is a critical element to reducing racism. In this chapter we identify key studies that support the hypothesis that group work and collaboration can instill group interdependence that is vital in overcoming discrimination and prejudice. In this chapter we address a key concept: A*ctivation* of potential skills in community projects with *Participation* among all group members = E*ducation* (**APE**).

In Chapter 9 we explore a rather unusual topic addressing the nonlinear relationship between technology and community service work. When used correctly, technology can immensely improve our ability in utilizing community service work principles with ethnically diverse groups. However, we are finding that greater technology use can also significantly alienate groups (and individuals) from each other. Technology is having a greater alienation impact on groups that ultimately influences how ethnically diverse groups interrelate. Community service work can help bridge this gap by relying on our basic and "technologically free" skills.

In Chapter 10, we set out the increasingly difficult paradox that is experienced by new immigrant groups: How to integrate and assimilate within the "dominant" group without compromising one's own cultural heritage and pride. In this chapter, we offer several examples for new groups to share their ideas, cultural heritage and history with others within the community as an effective measure that facilitates group cohesion, regardless of ethnic backgrounds and heritages.

Chapter 11 is concerned with how hate crimes may develop through communities that lack effective integration strategies and how we may help individuals communication. In a disturbing trend that actually inspired the thesis of this text, we explore the significant increases in hate crimes and how these crimes are affecting younger populations.

Chapter 12 looks at the issue of a "critical period" relative to the development of community service learning principles— in other words, does a (limited) time frame exist where the principles of community service learning develop most efficiently? If this is true, then what are the ages when community service learning principles should be implemented? For example, can community service learning work be "taught" to younger children? Can community service learning principles provide adolescents with a form of an identity and purpose? Can community service work help alleviate the common "mid-life crisis" that we see in middle adulthood and still provide meaning into late adulthood?

In Appendix A, Dr. Norma Espinosa Parker, a Cuban immigrant who teaches Spanish at El Camino College Compton Center, offers some insight relative to her views addressing immigration and assimilation within the dominant culture in the United States.

Why This Book Is Relevant

We are already beginning to see the disturbing signs of a lack of integration or assimilation in high schools and even grade schools where students often engage in institutionalized forms of racism and prejudice. We can also see the disturbing effects of individuals who lack any experiences and opportunities in sharing resources and activities via community service work. Typically these individuals engage in behaviors that are highly egoistic and reflect a "self-entitlement" attitude — expecting the community and others to provide the things that they should be providing to others. In many cases violence has erupted on school campuses due to long simmering feuds based on color and ethnicity. Often conflicts emerge simply as a consequence of perceived differences based on ethnicity and cultural beliefs.

Our schools and communities are rapidly becoming ticking time bombs based on an inability to promote effective dialogue and interaction among ethnically diverse student groups. Without some form of a comprehensive program that actively organizes and encourages students to interact and assimilate with each other, they will remain ethnically polarized. Ethnic polarization is the first step that leads to animosity, then anger towards ethnically diverse groups, and then ultimately ethnic hate crimes.

Bridging Ethnic and Cultural Divides

We have tried to link the important principles of community service work with the important theoretical constructs of cross-cultural psychology. Cross-cultural psychology is the scientific study of culturally diverse groups and the behaviors that develop from those groups within society and the community. Cross-cultural psychology helps us to improve our understanding of diversity and to better understand the dynamics of ethnically diverse groups who comprise the community itself.

Cross-cultural psychology also helps to understand our own behaviors in relation to groups who may be different from us relative to race, gender, economic class and religion. Community service learning principles and community service work activities are both effective methods to improve how members of different ethnic groups can improve the context of their relationships by allowing all groups to work towards a common goal. We will discuss specific methods how community service work can actually reduce prejudice and ethnocentrism as well as simultaneously improve communication among ethnically diverse groups.

It is common for individuals to react initially with some discomfort or anxiety when exposed to new situations with individuals that we are not familiar with. Some recent research may suggest that there may even be some evolutionary adaptive mechanism among humans that makes them predisposed (initially) to identify with other individuals who show more phenotypical or physical similarities, such as hair color and skin color (Buss, 2000). However, humans evolved with a need to survive as the strongest instinct, and when we develop groups based on one need (survival) that single need brings all persons together as an effective strategy to form interdependency. This key concept, interdependency, is the single most important factor relative to how ethnically diverse members of a community will establish positive relationships with each other. Without a common link or need that binds us all together (i.e., safety, food, or protection from the elements), our relationships will remain superficial and potentially destructive.

Race, culture, and economic class are increasingly characterizing the society in which we live in today. While most would agree that as societies are becoming increasingly more ethnically diverse, our ability to effectively engage in dialogue with others and interact with ethnically diverse individuals is becoming more difficult. Different groups of people from different geographic regions often have unique cultural values, dialogues, and patterns of behaviors that must be effectively explored in order to understand the unique characteristics of individual behavior. Often the best way to understand people to consider the environment in which they live. Only then do we have the context to understand individual behaviors and the behaviors of the group as well.

The value of diversity is only effective and educational when groups actually understand and communicate effectively among one another. Unfortunately, a common problem that often arises in multiethnic society (or any community where differences exist) is stereotyping. Stereotyping refers to attributing common characteristics (often negative characteristics) to all groups of individuals who share a common ethnic heritage or culture. We will explore the reasons how and why stereotypes develop and how to reduce stereotypes in our society.

Stereotypes really develop from what social psychologists refer to as the "cognitive miser" effect — we attribute the same characteristics to all members of a particular group. A cognitive miser is someone who likes to think as little as possible — thus attributing the same characteristics to all individual members of a group. To actually treat individuals as unique and separate persons and recognize that their behaviors may in fact contradict common stereotypes actually requires more mental effort — but this "mental effort" is precisely what we need to be doing more of if we ever really are serious about improving the quality of living in multiethnic society and reducing stereotypes. Polarization refers to the tendency for groups to remain homogeneous to avoid assimilation with other different groups of individuals (i.e., differences based on race, gender or religion). The purpose of this text is to offer the student a comprehensive description of effective collaborative skills that will facilitate interaction and an understanding of individuals who may have different backgrounds from our own.

We hope to use much of our own empirical research to create a text that addresses effective strategies that will facilitate interaction and communication among different ethnic groups in our society today. We should not only "tolerate" others who may be of different race or ethnicity from us but embrace these differences to help create a stronger and more enriched society for everyone. Clearly, we can interact more effectively and harmoniously than just "tolerating" each other — indeed, we can embrace each other by celebrating the diversity that makes our communities and societies so unique. The lack of assimilation among ethnically diverse communities sets the stage for serious future problems — such as prejudice, discrimination and in some cases even violence. Societies clearly need to be more proactive in their efforts to reduce problems that are characterized by stereotypes and poor communication between ethnically diverse groups. We feel that it is now more critical than ever to implement strategies within our own community that will facilitate assimilation and integration among ethnically diverse groups.

There are many things that we can *all* do to improve group interaction and communication among ethnically diverse groups in our society. Until now, these skills and techniques in improving dialogue between ethnic groups have largely remained ignored, with chances of inter-group assimilation occurring by random events or chance. However, given the increasing range of diversity that is currently growing within most communities today, it is imperative that we take a more proactive approach in finding ways for culturally diverse groups with various ethnic backgrounds to interact prosocially for the common good of the entire group. Perhaps one of the most important topics addressed in this text is the realization that we are a diverse community that essentially needs each other. Without understanding cooperative skills that clearly facilitate interaction among various ethnically and economically diverse groups, our culture will clearly perish. We hope to help all individuals discover by reading this text their own needs in cooperation and understanding members of diverse communities. When our community becomes strengthened by cooperative and community service work, then we become strengthened as well.

The potential to achieve these goals exists within each of us and will become realized only when we rediscover the inherent strengths of diversity and authentic power that we can all share when we work together through community service learning principles. We hope that you will read this book and discover the potential that community service work offers members of ethnically diverse groups to achieve common goals through interdependency.

1

Community Service Work in Compton College

Bringing People Together via Gardening Work

Think back about the last time that you engaged in some type of volunteer or community service work — how did that experience make you feel? Perhaps your community service work provided you with a sense of purpose in helping others. Perhaps you felt needed or you felt as though you were making some type of an important contribution to a greater cause? Did you feel better about yourself because you were able to help others without any expectation or reward in return? These are just some of the reasons why community service work is quickly becoming a popular activity among people from all different backgrounds and walks of life.

If you are like most people, your experiences were very positive in helping and working with others within your community. Additionally, your community service work and volunteer efforts were probably so rewarding that you were likely to repeat these behaviors— which is absolutely critical in achieving the true sense of "community" and growth. What you probably did not ask yourself is why you felt better about yourself in engaging in community service and volunteer work. Most people actually prefer to help others in a community setting because it helps the group as a whole and fosters a key ingredient in human interaction — interdependency. In this text we underscore the need and the importance in establishing positive interethnic interaction through our innate drive to work cooperatively with others. We focus exclusively through one technique —community service work — as a critical method in realizing our goals of interdependency.

We will also address the psychological importance and the personal

11

value that we all need to experience when engaging in any type of community service work. Community service work (CSW) is described here as any type of civic or community engagement where individuals combine their efforts with others for a public or community service such as education institutions (i.e., improving schools, parks or recreational areas for children). Community service work and civic engagement is more than just helping out people in your community; it is a necessary activity that all people need to experience in order to achieve maximum fulfillment in their lives.

How important is it to you to be able to contribute towards your community, your school, or your work environment? Often we take these things for granted, but recent research (Ferber, 2007) suggests that how we contribute to our community has important ramifications in terms of not only how we feel about ourselves but also how we feel and interact with others from different cultures. Communities that provide opportunities for individual members to contribute to the development and growth of the community itself (i.e., volunteer activities) typically result in greater civic unity and pride among the members. Therefore, in order for people to feel that they belong to the community or to be a part of society, they need to be contributing to that group in some way.

Community service work and the numerous benefits that are associated with community service work are becoming increasingly popular among people from all backgrounds who are also from diverse environments because it brings people together in a positive and dynamic way. People are beginning to discover the tremendous and dynamic value and importance in having ethnically and socioeconomically diverse groups of people (different groups of people based on ethnic, religious or economic backgrounds) work towards common goals.

Realizing Individual Strengths through Group Work

The motive and the impetus in writing this book is based primarily on our experiences in working with a vast mix of ethnically diverse students at Compton Community College working together with other students and community members for a common goal and purpose: to improve their school and transform it into an educational environment that they could feel proud of. The advantages of community service are numerous, and recently researchers have identified community service work and engagement as a highly effective technique in improving interethnic group behaviors and higher education (Hoffman & Wallach, 2006) as well as reducing self-entitlement and individualistic attitudes (Hoffman & Wallach, 2007).

Beginning in 2000, our research has focused on how individuals within the community and students in higher education respond to collective group work and community service work. My colleagues and I have noticed a disturbing trend within the last 20 to 30 years, a growing trend towards individualistic needs overshadowing the importance of collective group work. We now live in an era where individual success is tantamount to everything, and the merits of group work are secondary to the glitter of individual success. A consistent theme throughout our research addresses a very basic and evolutionary need for people to work cooperatively together on mutually beneficial projects. Unfortunately, however, as increases in technology develop within a highly developed individualistic culture, there are fewer and fewer opportunities for individuals to work together collectively and cooperatively. Our research in community service work has provided a dynamic opportunity for students at various levels (community colleges, state universities and graduate students) to work cooperatively in improving a campus environment in south Los Angeles (Compton Community College).

While the campus itself was clearly revitalized and much improved, perhaps a greater advantage to the community service project was in the transformation of the relationships among the students who had actually participated in the activity. The interaction and communication among all of the students had increased significantly, from an initial tendency towards ethnic polarization to a composed group effort, where each participant realized that they were involved in a cooperative assignment that was designed to improve the campus of the community college. We attributed this dramatic positive improvement in interaction to the psychological and dynamic effect of interdependence. Interdependence is only achieved when mutually dependent relationships (i.e., different groups of people working towards a common goal) are created and people realize that success is only achieved with the combined efforts of all people. When the participants in the community service project realized that they were capable of completing their goals only when they worked together, their relationships significantly improved. Improvements in relationships were defined as increased communication among each participant and reductions in negative stereotypes and ethnocentrism. Additionally, when people realize that they are capable of making positive contributions to the group or to the community, prosocial attitudes increase and aggressive behaviors (i.e., reduced ethnic conflict) significantly decrease. Recent research shows that communities that combine social learning theory techniques emphasizing positive behaviors, childhood and adolescent antisocial behaviors significantly decrease (Kazdin, 2003a).

The effect of community service work was also successful in influencing a greater transfer rate among the Compton Community College students to higher educational institutions, such as the California State University or the University of California systems. Because the community college students now had greater access and exposure to the California State University Northridge (CSUN) mentors, they were able to get the vital information needed to help them make successful transfers to the four-year university system. For example, mentors provided the community college students with applications and information for easy transition, but perhaps more importantly, the CSUN mentors themselves were positive role models that encouraged the community college students to continue their education. Traditionally Compton Community College students have had a low successful transition into higher educational institutions (i.e., four-year colleges or universities), in some cases as low as 10 percent to 15 percent successful transition. Since the development of the community service program at Compton Community College in 2000, student transition to the university level has significantly increased. Critical to the results of our community service work, we attribute this improvement in transition primarily due to the increased contact that the community college students had while participating in the community service program with the CSUN student mentors. The CSUN student mentors challenged the community college students to continue their education, and described higher education as a viable option that they were capable of achieving. This would have been virtually impossible without the unique working environment that the community service gardening program had provided.

Many people have expressed interest in community service and have asked the question how community engagement influences the relationships that people have with each other. To answer this question we need to describe how a gardening program at Compton Community College has really influenced the development of this text, addressing the numerous psychosocial and individual psychological benefits of community service work. Our experiences and research into the benefits of community service work began essentially as a short project designed to improve a community college such as Compton College. Compton College is one of the oldest community colleges in the United States and was established in 1927. The college over the years has seen many changes on the campus and among the students, and within the last 10 to 15 years declined in enrollment. The campus experienced financial cuts that left the physical appearance in an obvious state of disrepair. Most noticeable was the actual student area where the students would meet and interact socially. Litter was strewn about the area from nearby vending machines and the physical appearance (i.e., shrubs were growing wild and grass was uncut) was unkempt and a blight to the environment.

In 2000, some of the faculty at Compton College created a grassroots effort that was designed to improve the physical appearance of the campus. Many faculty volunteered their time off and began a gardening program, planting fruit trees, vegetables and flowers in the student garden area. As the students gradually observed the positive transformation and literal renaissance, they too became involved and began volunteering their time in weeding, planting and improving the area. Faculty wrote grants that provided the materials needed for the improvements, and within three to five years, the entire garden area (over three acres) underwent a remarkable transformation — it was beautiful. More important, however, were the dramatic psychosocial changes that we experienced among students working in the community service project. Over the years several empirical studies were addressed as a means of determining the viability and effectiveness of community service work and interethnic behaviors and reducing ethnocentric ideology (Hoffman, 2007c).

The community college students who worked with the CSUN mentors showed higher scores in self-esteem and self-efficacy after participating in the community service project. The students often formed positive bonds with their mentors and developed the self-confidence to make the educational transition to the CSU level. Additionally, many of the community college students felt more empowered and in control of the events that affected their lives, including significant improvements in internal attribution and self-efficacy. The increases in the perception of control over events in their lives were directly attributed to the positive experiences that the students encountered with the mentors in the community service activities. As the Compton Community College students increased their activities in the community service project, they became more confident of their educational futures and of transferring to four-year colleges and universities. The mentoring relationship with the community college students was a vital component of the community service project because it served as a bond of trust and support that stayed with the each student throughout the community service project.

Humans are social creatures and many of our activities involve working with each other in cooperative relationships and group-related projects. These projects may involve social relationships (i.e., a group of friends spending time with each other) or the relationships may be more goal-oriented and professional in nature. A "mentoring relationship" refers to some type of an educational relationship (usually between two people) where one individual learns and gains information from another person with specific types of experience. The mentor is the teacher, and the learner is the student — but in most cases individuals within this context learn and develop from each other. Interaction, communication, warmth, trust and dialogue are just some of the critical components that go into a successful mentoring relationship.

The most effective mentors, however, are those individuals who inspire learning and foster positive relationships with others by way of example. Effective mentors show students that they have the capacity to learn a variety of skills not by providing answers, but in showing students how to discover solutions on their own. Finally, effective mentoring means building a trusting and positive environment where support and communication remain constant throughout the relationship. Often, effective mentoring is characterized by learning that reciprocal — the mentor learns as much from the student as the student learns from his or her mentor.

The mentoring relationship can be a very successful learning relationship because it is highly beneficial and rewarding to both persons (community college students and their mentors who also happen to be students), as individuals typically enjoy both being the provider of information as well as the learner in new types of situations. Often, mentors report that the single most meaningful interaction and relationship with students is in the process of providing information to the student and seeing how the student learns and grows from the experience. Individuals who have not been afforded the opportunity of community service work and mentoring typically may not be aware of the tremendous rewards and satisfactions that are gained in making substantial contributions to the community. Indeed, all too often in a society we emphasize the value of any experience in terms of financial or monetary gain to the individual. In the individualistic culture, children quickly learn that things that are associated with monetary value are the greatest rewards, and that it is better to receive from the institution or community rather than to make contributions.

The benefits of community service work are that they allow individuals to experience deep interpersonal and intrapersonal positive experiences that clearly transcend superficial relationships that are unfortunately common today. These superficial relationships are clearly more evident in highly individualistic cultures that seem to emphasize personal self-worth that is based on competition, success and monetary income. Our individualistically oriented culture today is replete with media, advertisements, movie stars, and even sports heroes emphasizing the importance of *individual* performance and *individual* success. Meaning and identity in one's life is typically derived from achieving or winning something (usually with the assistance from others) with little or no investment in the group or community. Meaning, success and value within the individualistic culture are also highly dependent upon cosmetic or physically attractive characteristics that often have little influence on the true character of the individual. We base success on how the group or community can add to the development to the individual rather than asking how the individual can add to the development of the community at large. In our society today we measure meaning and success typically by competition and individual success, with little regard to the community that helped the individual in the beginning of his or her life. From this type of culture, individuals quickly develop an expectation of self-entitlement from others as a means of contributing to their own personal and individual identity.

This self-entitlement culture that we are talking about is actually the antithesis of community service work, where individuals are encouraged to make contributions to the larger community with no expectation of receiving compensation. Only when members of this type of a community can make a personal sacrifice to the community and can experience the intrinsic value of volunteerism and community service will the culture of self-entitlement cease to exist. Unfortunately, within the individualistic culture the emphasis is on the individual and how the group can serve the needs of the individual. Expectations for the group to serve the individual gradually develop into the self-entitlement culture that erodes the benefits of community service work.

Mentoring and Gardening within a Community Service Program

Recently the benefits of mentoring relationships relative to academic and educational improvements have been discovered as very instrumental in teaching individuals skills in a variety of community activities within unorthodox environments. When students work with their mentors in different types of environments (such as an outdoor gardening program) the quality of learning is enhanced and can actually motivate students to become more actively involved in community service projects. The principles of community service learning can be applied in either traditional academic environments (such as a classroom) or outdoor environments (such as garden areas). Mentoring is a very powerful tool that can actually be implemented within the group dynamic and can help individuals to discover their strengths and skills under the direction of their mentors.

Perhaps the single greatest benefit to mentoring within a community service program such as gardening activities is that the mentor actively becomes involved with students and all individuals work towards a common goal. When students see their mentors actively participating in a variety of community service programs, it serves to "legitimize" the activity and provides authenticity to the experience by their seeing all persons becoming actively involved. Furthermore, when the community college students see their work gradually becoming successful in creating a beautiful campus environment, they become more empowered to begin other projects and feel successful in completing them. Self-efficacy (perceptions of successful task accomplishment) relative to gardening as well as academic work (academic self-efficacy) also was significantly increased for all of the participants working in the gardening program.

Teacher Involvement
in Community Service Work

It is common to hear teachers and educators discuss the importance of being "environmentally friendly" and proactive in protecting our environment. However, it is not so common to see teachers and educators giving up a weekend to participate in a program to clean parks and recreation areas. In other words, are the teachers actually practicing their individual philosophy, or what is commonly referred to as "walking the walk"? The mentors and teachers that actually participate in these community service programs are sending a valuable message to the students that they serve — that they believe in the community service programs enough to make the commitments to participate in them. In the current study addressing community service work and the student perceptions of the importance of the volunteer work, students reported that "working with the teacher and mentors were very important" in how they responded to participating in the project. This form of empirical research is best described as "action-oriented" research, as it involves a dynamic relationship between the individuals who comprise the group and the work that is driven to improve a community facility or activity. It is always easier to complete a manual task when there are others there to help, and when the community college students actually began working, they commented frequently "how much fun" they were having in "discovering that gardening is exciting work."

The "exciting work" that these students were commenting on was the fact that they discovered a unique source of empowerment in working with other students of different races, mentors as well as their teacher. Working together, no matter how mundane the task, creates an incredible sense of potential to achieve goals. Furthermore, having persons of authority, such as the professor or instructor of the class, created a strong sense of legitimacy that community service work was a unique and special time to work together to create something beautiful for all persons to experience within the community.

A mentor can be described in many ways and used in many different types of contexts. Our definition of community service mentoring is "a relationship between two people that is based on trust, guidance and experience, where *both* individuals gain knowledge and insight based on their learning experiences within the environment." Mentoring relationships are productive in the sense that the mentors are providing valuable skills to the community college students, such as information relative to psychology, successful tips and techniques for success in preparing for higher education, and assistance in the transferal to higher education (i.e., providing brochures to various universities, applications, meeting new professors, etc.). Mentoring and group process are related and very productive when used together, as mentors who are trained within a specific area (i.e., as tutors in psychological theory, gardening skills, etc.) can help students not only improve in their academic performance, but can also increase academic self-efficacy (perceptions of future skills) and can improve interethnic assimilation and interaction. Mentors essentially provide a positive learning environment that allows the community college students an opportunity to discover their aptitudes relative to academic work while completing a community gardening program. In one study addressing the benefits of the community service work, CSUN mentors helped several community college students to successfully transition into higher educational institutions. This increase in successful educational transition was primarily a result of the positive relationships that were developed in the course of the community service work (Hoffman, 2004).

Community service programs that utilize the services of mentors may be implemented in a broad range of different types of service environments. In some cases (such as the present one), community service programs are designed to improve the physical structure and appearance of various public agencies serving underrepresented groups, such as a community college. As the community service program develops, students and mentors work essentially as one team in achieving two critical goals:

(a) Improving the physical appearance of the community college itself and

(b) Improving the academic skills and future of the community college student through the facilitation in transferring to higher educational institutions.

Our current study investigates a community service project involving underrepresented community college students and mentors from a four-year state university in a campus gardening program. What makes this program especially important is that the community college students need direction and support in their efforts to transfer to higher educational institutions, and the mentors were capable of providing this important function. The mentors earned credits towards their graduation requirements and volunteered their time (every Saturday morning from 7:00 A.M. to noon) in improving the physical structure of a community college. The community college predominantly serves underrepresented students (60 percent Hispanic students and approximately 40 percent African American students) and is a vital asset and resource to a limited environment with few resources for the inhabitants of the community.

The value of group process involving mentors and the benefits that are available not only for the mentors, but the students and the community, are numerous. Here are some examples of the benefits of a community service mentoring program:

Groups Can Function Best When

• Individuals are placed in a reciprocal relationship where each can help each other — in this way, interdependency is achieved;

- Mentors are placed in a volunteer — instruction relationship with students;
- Self-esteem and commitment to community service increases when mentors experience positive growth and change with students;
- When relationships are productive, both mentors and students can see their progress by the work as a team. Interdependency and positive growth can only occur in a community service program when both student and mentor realize similar goals and can understand achieving these goals means working together.

The primary educational and instructional value of the mentoring program involves the dynamic relationship between the mentors and the community college students, where several mentors (n = 10) have been working with the community college students over a period of one academic semester (approximately sixteen weeks). The mentors instruct and work with the community college students in terms of planting flowers, vegetables, and citrus trees that have been provided through a state grant. Additionally, the crux of the study involves the dynamic interactive relationship between the mentors and community college students as they continue working together. Positive relationships are formed and established throughout the semester and grow stronger as weeks continue — the mentors are actually helping to establish the long term educational plans of the community college students by helping them in their academic work and determining their future plans relative to psychology.

Often, these positive mentoring relationships that were originally established through community service work continued long after the program was completed. It is not uncommon, for example, to have many students who have participated in the community service work program to come by the campus to volunteer their time and effort again and meet new students.

For many of the El Camino College — Compton Center students, they are first generation students who are attending college for the first time and are balancing jobs and school as well as trying to support their families. The actual successful transfer rate to higher education has been very low, with only 5 to 10 percent actually transferring to higher education. We have been discussing the vital role that group process plays in determining and shaping how individuals from different ethnic groups relate to each other. Group process depends on one vital key — interdependency. Interdependency can only develop with trust, communication and a commitment from all members that they will work and complete their fair share of the work load. When individuals are placed in situations where they all need something together, such as a grade for a class, a verdict in a court room, or a flower and vegetable garden, their attitudes towards each other can improve significantly.

In this chapter we have focused on the unique and dynamic relationship between mentors and community college students within a community service gardening program. We have also focused on the potential numerous benefits that these mentoring programs can provide to students, the mentors, and the community itself. The concept relative to mentoring is rapidly becoming very popular among teachers and educators, as mentoring can provide direction, unity and productivity all within a very positive environment among group members. Group mentors can also provide supervision and assistance to other individuals within the group, depending on the nature and purpose of the group. Mentors are defined here as experienced student advisors providing direction to the academic and educational future of community college students. In our current program addressing community service work, several California State University Northridge students and Pepperdine University graduate students who were currently enrolled in a research design course and social psychology course volunteered to serve as student mentors to ethnically diverse community college students who were interested in transferring to higher educational institutions.

The gardening program typically involved one academic semester where ten students served as mentors from CSUN and Pepperdine University. The mentors volunteered to work Saturdays from 7:00 am to 12:00 noon with ethnically diverse community college students (n = 30). The main purpose of the mentoring program was to help improve the transfer rate of the community college students into a four-year college or university. The purpose of the mentors was to first establish a positive relationship (i.e., one which would enhance communication) with them through working in a community garden.

The mentors worked together with the community college students, planting flowers, pulling weeds, watering, and engaging in several tasks throughout the day to improve the physical appearance of the college itself. One may ask what planting flowers and vegetables has to do with successful academic transfer to higher education, and the answer is something that we have been addressing throughout this text: interdependency. When the community college students at Compton College worked in the garden with the mentors, they realized that there were many things that each of them had in common — a shared interest in psychology, interests in educational research in psychology, outdoor activities such as the gardening program, and so on. The discovery of shared interests and common goals helped both groups of students (mentors and community college students) develop a positive working relationship that in turn influenced the community college students to transfer to higher education.

Similarly, the mentors discovered in their work with the community college students their interest in working with underrepresented students and the intrinsic value and benefits of volunteer and community service work. Stated simply, both groups of students were gaining from each other and valued their experiences with each other. As time progressed, this positive relationship developed further, and the bond of trust and interdependency expanded into a unique and supportive friendship and positive educational relationship. The "interdependency" we refer to provide the impetus and motivation to keep working in the community service gardening program as students realized that they had much to gain from each other. We argue in our research that the smaller phenomena of interdependency that developed in our community service program with the mentors and community college students are precisely the kinds of things that our society needs to be doing more of if we truly wish to decrease conflict among ethnic groups. The interdependent experience that the students shared with each other provided the very substance of what made the community service program so successful.

Collective versus Individualistic Societies Influencing Community Service Work

Societies and communities today are failing our students by not providing adequate opportunities to engage in community service work. Individuals need to be shown and demonstrated (by way of example through the mentor's actual behaviors) the benefits and rewards of making sacrifices and volunteer work devoted to improving the community at large. Unfortunately, many students are asking, "What can the community provide for me?" or "What do I get out of this?" when they should be more concerned with what contributions they can make to the community or to less fortunate persons in society. We will discuss in more detail the effects of the collectivistic and individualistic culture on behaviors among students participating in the community service program in chapter seven.

When students can see that the mentor they are working with has made an authentic investment in them as a person and as a unique individual, they will be motivated to continue this work in the future with other community service work. More importantly, the students are provided with a mechanism to achieve a sense of belonging and unconditional acceptance through their work with the mentor and community service work. Community service work is therefore more about trust and establishing positive relationships in our work with others, and seeing the benefits to the schools and communities as our work progresses. It is this fundamental belief that all humans need the opportunity to provide something of value in terms of experiences and positive relationships that are critical in maintaining a healthy and productive community.

When each of the mentors developed their working relationship with the community college students through the gardening program, a bond of trust and communication developed through their work with each other. The relationship and trust between the community college students and the CSUN / Pepperdine University mentors proved to be a critical asset to the success of the community service program. The community college students developed a more positive sense of self and academic self-efficacy through their work with the mentors.

Comments by
Community Service Mentors

- **Michelle:** "I enjoy working with the students because I learn more from them — it is very rewarding for me to see how my efforts have made positive changes in someone's life."
- **Elizabeth:** "I never have had much experience in working with diverse groups, and most of the time I spent my Saturday mornings at my house just reading the newspaper. I really find it very rewarding to be doing something proactive in helping others, and teaching others the benefits of gardening and community service work."
- **James:** "One of the most exciting things that I have ever done was work as a mentor. It is particularly exciting for me because I can directly see the positive changes that I am making on a daily basis. Helping people and seeing how their behaviors improve is everything I had hoped for in the field of psychology…. I just never realized that I could experience something like this in a community service gardening program."
- **Raya:** "It just makes me feel good to know that I am doing the right thing

and helping people who are less fortunate than me. The more I see how my work is making a positive change in people's lives, the more motivated I become to continue my [service learning] work."

Comments by Community College Students Working with the Mentors

- **Keisha:** "When I was working with the CSUN mentors I was able to find out how I could apply for grants and scholarships. Without some type of financial support, I would not be able to continue my education past Compton College.... I really enjoyed being able to talk to the mentors while we were all gardening. I was able to see that there are many things that I can do in psychology when I transfer to a CSU college."
- **Carlos:** "Just after a few weeks I realized that I now want to change my major from welding to psychology. Working with the CSUN and Pepperdine folks [mentors] helped me to realize that my goals are really now working with people, just like they have worked with us. It has been a great program for me."
- **Mayra:** "The gardening program has been a great way for me to meet other people with interests in psychology. I really liked the fact that all groups of people were working together.... [E]veryone got along because we just wanted to improve the college. It has been a nice experience for me. I take these experiences home and share them with my family."

2

Group Work as a Necessary Factor of Human Evolution

WORK COOPERATIVELY TOGETHER OR PERISH

Humans evolved millions of years ago with one very basic and universal motive: survival. Our world — the one we have evolved from and continue to evolve in — was an especially hostile, cold and unfriendly place to live. Any characteristic that proved to be particularly useful and adaptive was incorporated into the group dynamic that was used and shared by all members, and anything (including persons) that proved maladaptive to the group integrity and structure *ipso facto* did not survive — there were no exceptions. Differences (whether phenotypical or genotypical) were perceived as foreign and a threat to the group safety. Individuals who did not work collectively and share responsibilities that were central to survival were either expelled from the group as pariahs, or in some cases even murdered. There were no appeals systems or democracy designed for group fairness.

Old sayings or aphorisms ring true for social events: avoid particularly contentious topics (i.e., religion and politics) and people are significantly more likely to avoid conflict and enjoy each other's company. Even friendly and "light-hearted" discussions that begin innocuously enough often gradually devolve into heated arguments and discord that leads to resentment. Sometimes this resentment is simply based on misunderstandings; other times, however, the understanding is all too clear and the conflict is based on basic and primary fundamental values. Perhaps our strong need for consensus on particularly divisive topics, such as religion or politics, is why many individuals respond in especially vitriolic and

26

passionate ways during social gatherings. Strong political or religious differences mark profound differences in cultural values and a basic sense of "right versus wrong"—and individuals who strongly differ from us in this regard may actually be triggering a very deep-seated and deep-rooted belief system from our own evolutionary history. Differences in these basic belief systems millions of years ago created a vulnerability and weakness to the group or clan, and this basic need for some consensus is probably still with many people today.

Predators, cold temperatures, extreme heat and drought made daily living a constant challenge. If humans were to exist in these extremely difficult conditions, there was one thing above all that was most critical to our survival—cooperation among members and interdependency. Most anthropologists agree that our Neanderthal ancestry lived primarily in small clans, usually numbering only eight to twenty, and were nomadic, often roaming up to 10, 15 and even 20 miles daily in search of food. This hostile and unforgiving environment made survival critical — interdependency.

Most research psychologists who specialize in adaptation and evolutionary psychology now agree that there have been many characteristics that were critical to our survival millions of years ago that still have a profound influence on our behaviors today. How we relate to others, our cooperative behaviors and our styles of communication are three very good examples of adaptive behaviors that were necessary for our own survival. Millions of years ago the determining factor regarding our survival was what we could have contributed to the group or clan. Some individuals (typically males) were expert in hunting and catching game as a primary food source, and others were expert in obtaining other sources of foods, such as fruit, vegetables and various nuts (typically female). Some individuals prepared foods, some tended to children, and some gathered fresh water, and so on.

The critical feature of each of these small groups (or clans) was that each member contributed to the overall welfare of the group — the more individuals worked cooperatively together, the greater their individual chances of survival while remaining intact as a group. Groups that encourage all members to work together and focused on all inherent skills and attributes of individual members had the greatest advantages because the group itself was stronger and more resilient to threats, but more importantly individual members were happiest because they were contributing to the integrity and overall fitness of the group. This contribution provided a sense of belonging to the group and affirmation to the group ensuring safety in times of stress and danger.

Evolutionary Theory and Ethnic Polarization: Genetically Predisposed Preferences in Homogeneity

One characteristic that is commonly seen among groups of individuals today is what is referred to as "ethnic polarization." A group that shares common phenotypical and cultural characteristics and avoids interaction with other groups (often resulting in the development of ethnic enclaves) is characterized as ethnic polarization. A common problem that is demonstrated among "ethnically diverse" groups is simply the actual lack of diversity within the group itself. There appears to be (among many different groups) an initial preference or predispositions (at least initially) to identify with and to only associate with others who appear more like us. There does appear to be some evidence in our early evolutionary history that preferring those who phenotypically (i.e., physical or directly observable traits) appeared more like us tended to improve our chances of survival (Buss, 1999). Clans typically consisted of eight to twenty members. Millions of years ago, if a member of a clan wandered to a different territory or to a different clan where there may have been physical differences in their appearance, he or she may have been perceived as a threat to the safety or to the integrity to the clan and murdered.

These (albeit initial) preferences to those who appear more like us still remain with us today. Just go to any public area where there are different groups of people and typically you see persons of similar physical appearances initially congregate with each other. There are, however, many things that we can (and should) do to promote assimilation and integration with members of different ethnic and cultural backgrounds, and collaborative group work is perhaps the most effective.

The point is that when environments allow and even encourage all different group members to effectively contribute to the fitness and overall adaptation of the environment, all of these members who comprised the group felt needed and that they were serving some purpose. There was less of a need of aggression because individuals felt that they were proactive in their ability to contribute to the needs of the group. Many theorists who describe the humanistic view relative to behaviors argue that it is precisely this very need to contribute to the group and the need to be needed as the catalyst that promotes healthy interactions and exchanges in our society. Alfred Adler, Erikson and Carl Rogers all write about the essential need that all people have in identifying our unique and creative skills (i.e., "social interest") and contributing towards the community.

The humanistic model argues that all persons possess innate positive potential that is used to contribute to society and the community.

When individuals see how they literally "fit" within a community and feel that they have something of value to offer to others, a sense of *purpose* is established. The sense of purpose becomes manifested and developed only within the social context of the community itself: A need to be needed is developed. In a real sense, then, the humanistic perspective argues that *individual* identity is only achieved within the relationship and partnership of others, the essence of a true community. The foundation and basic principles of community service work have their roots firmly established in the evolutionary history of human behaviors. Humans have literally evolved for millions of years with a basic and innate need to contribute to their clan that ensured safety and adaptability for all members within the group itself. When we feel as though we have something of value to offer and contribute to the group, our existence within the group is justified. Additionally, when we realize our "fit and connectedness" within the group, our relationships with others becomes significantly and reciprocally more positive (Heine & Norenzayan, 2006).

In this way, we embody the collectivistic philosophy that we indeed are group or social creatures defined not only by our contributions to society, but also by the various types of things that we receive from others. This reciprocal relationship with others in our community provides a healthy balance of "give and take" or homeostasis that enables us to live productively with others. This need to be needed that serves as a function or purpose and aids in the group's survival is how we define interdependency and still remains critical today.

Those communities or societies that provide these activities for individual members (i.e., working in shelters to provide food for the needy, engaging in community service work, etc.) typically have the most efficient and prosocial communities today because members feel a need to contribute to help others. The need to help others and contribute to our society is thus inborn and we are genetically predisposed to carry out these behaviors in a social group (Trivers, 1990). To be deprived of these opportunities to engage in helpful activities with others creates an imbalanced community that is predisposed to socioeconomic imbalance, prejudice and discrimination. Cooperative group work is an effective way to organize the skills and talents of a variety of individuals to create projects that combine these skills into a superior project. Furthermore, cooperative group work facilitates the development of interdependency, which serves as the glue bringing diverse groups of individuals together.

As an illustrative example describing this concept, imagine the tens of thousands of individuals who are kept locked up in various prisons and jails throughout the country. We are not recommending nor are we suggesting simply releasing all of the offenders—that would be ridiculous and unsafe in any society. However, imagine if we could somehow utilize the tremendous resources that each individual has and somehow tap into this vital resource. We not only would be putting a vast resource to economic need, but we would also be playing a more effective role in true rehabilitation. Remembering what the psychosocial theorists argued, antisocial behavior and destruction are primarily caused by individuals not being afforded an opportunity to develop their true and inherent skills. Imagine for a moment the vast potential that is currently being locked up and going to waste. The more a community works towards utilizing skills among individuals who comprise the community, the less likely that community will have violent or antisocial behaviors.

Reciprocal Altruism: Beware of Those Who Bring Gifts!

The key to understanding and valuing each other is in knowing how we can all work together peacefully without conflict. The capacity to work cooperatively with each other was a tremendous advantage to our survival and in the long run improved our own capacity of reproductive fitness. What Robert Trivers (1990) refers to as "reciprocal altruism" supports this theory, as favors performed by one individual for another individual increased the likelihood of favors being done for you at some point in the future. Thus, the more cooperative you are with others and help them in a crisis situation, the more likely it is you will receive assistance in the future when needed. When individuals see that someone has previously helped them now needs assistance, they are significantly more likely to stop what they are doing and help. Thus, ultimately helping others in the long run is really more like helping oneself in terms of survival, and altruism quickly became a necessary feature among small groups of people living together.

Despite many skeptical opinions today, it is possible for groups to live and work together if certain conditions exist in society. Most of the successful societies that exist today offer educational opportunities for all individuals and provide wide employment opportunities for most individuals. When communities provide opportunities for individuals to excel and develop their skills and attributes, there are fewer reasons to engage in crime or other forms of antisocial behaviors. More importantly, individuals feel as though they are actually contributing to a social and economic purpose that provides them with a sense of purpose each day. Many psychologists that focus on human potential and relationships emphasize the need for an environment that allows individuals to work towards and maximize their personal and professional growth within the context of their relationships with others.

Alfred Adler (1929), Carl Rogers (1959) and Abraham Maslow (1968) are all excellent examples of humanistic theorists who have focused on positive human growth and personal development through various forms of crises that result in positive growth potential. Thus, current social problems such as ethnic violence, discrimination and ethnocentrism should be viewed as socially constructed problems that are *learned* in maladaptive environments. A fundamental belief shared by each of these theorists is that human nature never begins flawed, but rather becomes flawed through corrupted society and maladaptive environments. When individuals are provided with opportunities to work together (collaboratively) within the group, the development of group cohesiveness increases as does the development of human potential. People feel closer to each other when they work out problems together where each person feels capable of contributing to a specific solution. Group process and development can help to correct these problems by providing individuals with the key component — interdependency.

The important concept to understand is that of interdependency: knowing that we all have certain skills, traits and qualities that can enhance how we all live together. Think back to the last natural disaster — whether it was an earthquake, a flood or a tornado— and how people responded to each other. It really didn't matter what that person looked like, what particular religion he or she happened to belong to, or his or her economic class or gender. The point was that people were drawn together by a need, and when people work collectively together, the quality of living for future generations and ourselves rapidly increases. This was true over a million years ago as we evolved, and it remains true today.

Improving Education
via Collaborative Group Work

The need to provide and offer our skills in combination with our ability to receive help from others is what makes us unique social creatures. The dualistic need of contributing and receiving help from others is the foundation of what makes cooperative group work most effective. This unique reciprocal relationship that all people have is fundamental in the development of cooperative group work. When individuals feel that they have something valuable (i.e., a skill or a trade) that is unique to offer that can be used in an instrumental way, their overall subjective experiences in working with others significantly increases, regardless of the ethnicity or class of those individuals. In traditionally collectivistic societies and cultures, the group is the central focus of daily living. Individuals ask what they can provide for the group so all members within the group may benefit. Collectivistic philosophy is essentially a very unselfish and altruistic experience that emphasizes inner growth and a sense of purpose develops from contributing our skills to the group itself.

A collectivistic culture is one where all group members are encouraged to participate and share in the responsibility of a group or community goal. Collectivistic cultures allow individuals from various backgrounds to combine their skills and aptitudes with other persons to work on a mutual project. Often these projects completed by groups operating under a collectivistic culture are superior in many ways—combined efforts by many different persons allow for small groups to utilize their skills in a variety of ways.

Our culture within the United States unfortunately does not typically embrace or utilize this form of work ethic; we tend to be more individually oriented and focus more on individual achievements rather than on group-oriented achievements. Contrary to collectivistic theory, individuals who succeed by themselves are often rewarded and congratulated for working independently. Thus, we can see profound differences in how individuals value their relationships, success and accomplishments when comparing the individualistic and collectivistic cultures.

The individualistic culture is highly competitive, autonomous, and usually develops a norm of internality — assuming personal control over events within his or her life. Here, in our Western culture, we have emphasized the importance of individualism to the point where we have lost sight of the benefits of group work and conformity. Indeed, the term "conformity" itself conjures up negative images among most Westerners (Jellison & Green, 1981). Within the collectivistic culture, group work and conformity are key factors to personal growth and meaning. Success of the group is defined as individual success. Individual identity is defined through group participation. This is the key factor that makes cooperative work so important, not only in higher education, but in society in general because it provides the glue that holds societies together and allows them to function at optimum levels.

The Value of Collaborative Group Work

The inherent value and benefits of collaborative group work (when organized correctly) can be achieved within a variety of different types of environments, educational, professional and even personal relationships. To "collaborate," literally defined, refers to working together, usually in an intellectual manner. Instructors need to emphasize to students who are working in the classroom that they all have information and experiences vital and instrumental in completing their work. In classrooms where instructors use the educational principles of cooperative learning, students are organized into small ("collaborative") work groups and are given one assignment that is graded. When one grade is awarded to the entire group, all members ideally contribute relatively equally in the work. When all members work towards their individual achievement, the collective efforts of individuals work to the advantage of the entire group. All members must work together (thus forming interdependency with each other) if they hope to achieve a positive outcome for their assignment.

Typically the assignment covers important information and is written so that all students are capable of sharing their responses in a way that contributes to the development of the assignment. Additionally, usually one grade is awarded to each student who is in the group, thus serving as an effective incentive to ensure that all students are contributing relatively equally to the group project. Successful collaborative assignments encourage all students to share their information and to thus provide valuable input. This information makes the assignment academically more sound because the information is now coming from not one but three or four different sources. When the assignment in collaborative group work is appropriately constructed, all members comprising the group are afforded the opportunity to provide input and information critical to the completion of the assignment.

Often, the individual sources that comprise the group can include different perspectives, theories and views that are influenced by economic class, gender and ethnicity. What makes cooperative or collaborative group work very successful and popular is that all students are sharing and working together towards a mutual goal (i.e., getting a good grade on the project) and they have the autonomy to develop their project by utilizing all of the skills, experiences and knowledge base from each member. Thus, collaborative group projects inherently have the potential to produce far superior work than assignments that are completed individually or in more traditional styles.

The key point to emphasize here is that when people do pool together their skills, resources and efforts, the end result is almost always significantly more favorable than if people worked individually. However, this is precisely the problem in an individually oriented society. Our culture, unfortunately, does not encourage collaborative group efforts and we focus more on individual attention. Collaborative groups in higher education allow students to share their ideas and to help contribute exemplary work by utilizing all of the skills and aptitudes of group members.

Historically collectivistic cultures have embraced the concepts and practices of collaborative group work. Collectivistic cultures have emphasized the value and importance in group work and structure tasks in such a way that all individuals feel capable of contributing to the solution to a problem. While collectivistic cultures recognize the value of individual attention, there is a greater emphasis in terms of what *the group* can achieve rather than *groups of individuals*. The group itself is perceived as a single entity or an identity and is not typically perceived as a collection of separate individuals and identities. Collectivistic cultures have therefore emphasized (and capitalized on) the values of group conformity, concepts relative to interdependence, and cohesion as key factors not only towards group success, but individual happiness attained via working with the group (Triandis, 1990).

Limitations of the Individualistic Culture: Why the Lakers Could Not Win in 2007

We all want "winners" on our team representing who we are — no one wants to be considered a "loser" or even to participate on a losing team. This very powerful dynamic has strongly influenced the outcome of not only how sports are played, but also how we engage in education. When too many individuals focus on scoring the highest grade, the highest GPA, or simply performing well without understanding information, or, in Kobe Bryant's case, scoring the most points, we create environments that are highly competitive and the quality of education becomes compromised.

While the benefits to the individual are numerous and certainly possible, the overall potential benefits to the group itself become limited. In the corporate world, an individual who competes for a privileged position can maximize his or her benefits, but these benefits come from the collective efforts of all employees in the business. One person benefits from the collective efforts of the group. This principle can be very disastrous, especially if the individual may be in a particularly powerful position and is corrupt (i.e., Enron and corporate greed).

In the world of professional sports, athletes often are viewed as American royalty — they are internationally famous, usually very wealthy, and hugely popular among fans (certainly more so than politicians or teachers). How well (or poorly) an athlete plays can determine success or failure in competition. In the case of team sports, individuals (by definition) are supposed to work together and combine their strengths to defeat the opponent. A recurring problem, however, is when individuals within team sports begin to play as if they were the team itself. The virtue and strength of team sports is simply that — individuals combining their skills to create a very powerful team. Within the individualistic culture which is predominant in the Western hemisphere, an individual may be on a team sport, but unfortunately still play as an individual, ignoring the critical principles that make group process successful.

The famous Lakers basketball player Kobe Bryant may score 65 points a game or even over 80 points and improve his overall standing, but there is no guarantee that the team will benefit from his highly individualized performance or even have a winning season (i.e., there were several games during the 2007 season where Kobe Bryant scored over 50 or 60 points and the team still lost!). Consider the short-term versus long-term benefits of collectivism and individualism: In a highly individualistic performance, one may improve his or her skills with impressive points, but in the long run, the team itself becomes compromised because they are not afforded an opportunity to practice and develop their skills *as a team*. So, in plain and simple terms, while Kobe Bryant initially appears *individually* positive (i.e., media) for his unique performance, in the long run the team loses by not qualifying for the post-season and by other team members not benefiting from equal playing time. Additionally, individual dominance in a team sport prevents other talented younger players from developing their skills which, in the long run, may help overall team performance. (We will discuss more about individualistic and collectivistic cultures influencing group performance in chapter 8).

In similar situations involving individual cooperation in group work, if one student dominates the quality of work performance over other group members, then the progress and potential for learning within the group dynamic becomes limited. Conversely, when students ($n = 4$) in a small collaborative groups work interactively and interdependence is established within the group, then the group output and educational potential becomes maximized for all group members. In simple terms, when individuals within the group work cooperatively and collaboratively, then the capacity for gains among individuals increases exponentially.

The problem with a highly individualistic culture is not so much individual work per se, but rather an inability to appreciate the intrinsic value of collaborative group work as well as a failure in understanding the significantly more powerful effect of combining all pools of talent and aptitude, a term now referred to as "collective self-efficacy."

Collective self-efficacy refers to the concept that certain goals can be achieved only through the cooperation and collaboration of skills and talents contained within the group itself. Thus, political activism, group efforts designed to improve the environment and even success in sport competition are often only successful through collective self-efficacy. Using a more positive example of collective efforts and sports, the 2003 National Baseball League World Series champions Boston Red Sox were not expected to even earn a berth in the pennant. However, when the team members combined their skills collectively (they were all rookies), they were able to win the World Series by playing as a cooperative and supportive team. Thus, as groups of individuals begin to identify with each other and combine their skills as an effective unit, not only are they better equipped to achieve their goals, their perceptions of what they can actually accomplish significantly improve as well. The term "self-efficacy" refers to a belief in the ability to achieve a specific goal, and "collective efficacy" refers to groups of individuals (such as team members) believe in their capacity to achieve their goals as a single unit. Typically their belief systems become more positive about their outcomes and their identities even change—from individuals to teammates and group members.

In terms of modern education today, many students need to take on responsibility by themselves and receive recognition by themselves, where reliance on others is actually perceived as a negative feature or flaw. Part of the virtue and benefits of the collectivistic theory is that work that is completed individually is now shared with others to create a more balanced work that represents the efforts of the group itself. Educators and teachers who combine collaborative group work in the classroom in higher education consistently produce students with higher academic performance than teachers who choose more traditional methods of teaching (i.e., only lectures).

Characteristics of Group Development and Community Service Work

We have mentioned previously that collaborative group work is fundamentally superior in many ways in teaching and learning in higher education. Group work allows students to learn from each other and provide effective means of communication that can help to build work and research that utilizes the talents and all skills of members who comprise the group. Many of the advantages of collaborative group work are fundamental in the development of community service work. One similarity is that both styles of learning involve the distinct advantages of groups— people working together for a common purpose. In collaborative group work, typically assignments are completed within the classroom and involve three or four students sharing information together for one grade. Interdependency is achieved in collaborative group work as well, as each student knows that his or her grade is dependent on the other group members' performance.

The more each participant contributes and volunteers to the group project, the more likely the entire group will receive a desirable outcome. *Knowing that your individual outcome (i.e., a grade or completing a community project) is dependent on another person working cooperatively with you inherently brings the best out in all of us.* This is the thesis and *a priori* of community service work — when groups of people work cooperatively together for a common purpose. our goals are more readily achieved and (most importantly among ethnically diverse groups) our relationships with each other significantly improve as well. The same is true for community service work. A group of people work together for a common purpose and the end result is an improved and aesthetically pleasing community or civic area, educational institution or public park. Similar to the collaborative group project, the harder each individual works within the group, the more successful the group itself becomes.

One form of empirical research has been conducted by Bruce Tuckman (1965) that supports the hypothesis of group work and the five stages of group development: Orientation (forming); Conflict (storming); Structure (norming); Work (performing); and Dissolution (adjourning). Tuckman's research addresses the fundamental changes that occur and develop as groups experience growth with each other. All groups go through a process of fundamental psychodynamic change and development where members grow in their relationships with each other. The process of group development in community service work progresses from the initial phase where people are introduced to each other and then are assigned a group task. The process of achieving the group task collectively helps to foster interdependence among group member. Groups that are developed and engage in community service work also evolve in specific ways where members develop very positive relationships with each other. When people first meet each other for the first time, they tend to remain friendly and civil with each other — this first phase is referred to as the "friendly" phase — getting to know each other for the first time.

In our own research we present the "Five Fs of Group Process": The Friendly Phase, the Friction Phase, the Forming Phase, the Follow-through Phase, and the Finish Phase.

1. **The Friendly Phase:** people initially formulate relationships and try their best to get along with each other. In this beginning phase of group development, individuals meet each other for the first time and become oriented to the group process and overall function of the group itself;
2. **The Friction Phase:** group conflicts inevitably develop as important issues and important decisions become necessary;
3. **The Forming Phase:** The Forming Phase allows group members who are assigned a community service task to establish roles and individual responsibilities. Examples of these different types of dynamic changes include who the group leader(s) may be, how communication in the group is disseminated, and, in more general terms, how roles are assigned;
4. **The Follow-through Phase:** once the positions and the responsibilities of group members have been identified, the group is ready for the most important assignment — beginning the task and completing the task. In community service projects, these tasks are typically designed to improve a public area, a park, community college or educational institution that serves the needs of several members;
5. **The Finish Phase:** a positively motivated group is a very dynamic and powerful force where each individual member realizes that he or she can achieve many different tasks when all members work together. Because of the realization of the power that each group possesses in

community service work, it is often difficult for group members to realize that their mission and job is complete. Often, many of the students who have participated in community service projects remain in close contact with each other through the years. Additionally, it is not uncommon for many students who have participated in past community service projects to continue their volunteer work years later.

We will now briefly review how each stage of group development develops within a community service project:

The Friendly Phase: Getting to Know One Another

Before any group can begin work on a problem, members must first get to know one another and answer vital questions: Are they like us or different from us? How well can we communicate with the new group members? Do we have much in common with them? When students meet together for the first time in community service groups, they first evaluate each group member to identify what they appear to have in common with each other and what are the ostensible differences. Initially everyone appears to be friendly, helpful and cooperative. When groups first become organized, individuals need to introduce themselves to each other and "get to know" one another. While this common practice sounds appropriate, the problem is that different group members may be already positioning themselves for key positions within the group for power and control, so they may be projecting a somewhat "less authentic" perspective of who they truly are. In order for all groups to maximize their efficiency and become task-oriented, they must all first identify each other and realize each other's individual strengths and skills. When different members of the group are capable of assuming diverse and critical needs, the adaptiveness and ultimately the cohesiveness of the group increases, thereby ensuring the integrity of the group itself;

The Friction Phase: Conflicts within the Group Are Inevitable

A common assumption within group dynamics is that when groups form, people somehow tend to magically get along with no outward signs of conflict. Nothing could be further from the truth. People (at least initially when the groups form) engage in various forms of conflict quite frequently. Conflict is an inevitable part of forming human relationships, but what is critical in the phase of conflict is in having a better understanding of each other to facilitate future interaction. Groups, small or large, are typically inclined to experience some conflict as a means of establishing position and hierarchy. Conflict is a natural (and inevitable) part of life, but what is more important how we resolve the conflict as the group achieves its goals. When all members of the group realize that they need to work together and remain unified as a means to achieve their goals, conflicts are quickly resolved. In community service work, individuals realize that the only way goals (such as cleaning a park or planting a community garden) can be successfully achieved is through mutual and reciprocal cooperation.

Some of the more common conflicts include roles (i.e., who is the leader of the group and how are roles within the group identified or determined?). Once these inherent conflicts have been addressed through group work, the real work (structure) is about to begin. When individuals representing different ethnic groups are able to work together in a productive and highly communicative way, real solutions are possible. Solutions are only achieved, however, when all members who represent different groups realize that a singular problem affects all members of a society, and that when all members work cooperatively towards a solution, the end result is an improved society and community for all people. The key component during this second phase of group formation is that when conflict does occur, all members work out solutions together. This is critical so all group members realize effective problem solving solutions do exist and that they may be utilized during various phases of the group process.

Forming Roles and Establishing Structure within the Group

How the group is formed and how the roles are determined are critical elements to the overall success of the group itself. During the initial stages of group development, group members typically share ideas and discuss with one another their ideas, what they think they can contribute to the group, their advantages, strengths and so on. It is here that a critical element of both group development and community service work is achieved — individual group members assigning roles to the each other. The role assignments are not necessarily fixed; individuals may shift roles and assignments depending on the progress and gradual achievement of each goal. Members of the group now actually take on a different view of themselves, from an "individual" member to now being part of a collective group effort. The third phase of group development in community service work is the formation of group roles—individuals within the group are now perceived as being a part of something or a team component rather than an individual. Additionally, the identity of the individual now changes from a singular component of the group to an actual group member whose identity becomes the group itself. This transition of identity represents the collectivistic philosophy: group efforts are significantly more effective than an individual effort. The development of the formation phase also includes a critical element to community service work—identifying roles among each group member. Part of the unique advantage to community service work is that members within the group typically all possess various skills, many of them diverse skills that combine to create a unique and powerful force. The development of roles within the community service group allows individuals to identify their own unique skill that can add to the power of the group in achieving each goal.

Follow-Through Phase — Doing the Work!

Once the community service group has been identified and the roles of each group member have been determined, the real work is now about to unfold. The group is now ready to begin work in achieving their goals. In the gardening program at Compton Community College, the roles of group members were quickly established where the mentors helped students in planting flowers, trees, and shrubs. The work that is done in community gardening is actually shared by all group members, regardless of the particular role of the individual. A good example would include the professor or the teacher of the class assuming different roles. Many of the students who participated in the community service program indicated that they were surprised when they saw their teacher dressed in shorts and tennis shoes actively participating in the gardening process. The Follow-through Phase typically involves three steps:

1. Identifying what the goals are;
2. What is the best procedure in achieving the goal; and
3. Executing the procedure.

Finish Phase — Ending the Group Process

Some proponents of community service work and cooperative group work maintain that a group effort is never complete and that as long as there are people around there will always be opportunities for community engagement. All groups at some point complete their work and move on to new challenges and new goals. With some of the more successful and dynamic groups, termination can be very difficult. Many of the community service groups that have worked together for six, eight or even twelve months still remain in contact with each other. A highly successful group is one that is dynamic and where all members feel as though they are contributing towards a goal.

Community Service Work and Interethnic Relationships: We Can All Get Along!

In various levels of education a very popular and highly effective teaching mechanism that involves small or cooperative groups is that of interethnic collaborative group work. Numerous studies have been conducted that have identified educational strategies when teachers incorporate group work in the classroom. Group work not only allows students to learn more effectively from each other, they can use each other as effective partners to share information and create improved projects or term papers and use each other's personal experiences relative to their own backgrounds, which may also help to improve the overall educational experience.

In our own research we have identified yet another advantage to teachers who incorporate interethnic study groups with cooperative group assignments (Hoffman, 1995). The advantages to teachers who incorporate interethnic study groups in the classroom not only afford students better opportunities to process and retain information relevant to the course, they are also allowing students opportunities to engage in effective interactive techniques that have been shown to reduce ethnocentrism and debunk myths and stereotypes pertaining to different ethnics groups.

In environments where students of diverse ethnic groups often work and study together, those teachers who combine the groups to have students from different racial backgrounds are actually helping students to better understand each other from a cultural perspective as well as an academic perspective. The effects of collaborative group work among ethnically diverse groups of students are numerous, but perhaps the most positive aspects of this research show the significant reductions in ethnocentrism (beliefs in the superiority of one ethnic group over another) and significant increases in prosocial attitudes among diverse groups. Thus, academic performance improves when students are able to work together in cooperative groups because they are utilizing each other as academic resources and can review the material more effectively.

3

The Establishment of Roles within the Group

The moment groups have actually become established, things begin to change. Individuals will begin to interact and communicate with each other. In some groups, this form of interaction occurs smoothly and effortlessly; in other group situations, conflicts seem to emerge from the first day. Whatever the style of group interaction, these behaviors will soon determine how roles are established within the group and how individual strengths and skills develop. These skills and strengths within the group are critical and often determine whether or not the group will be able to achieve their goals. Thus, an *a priori* theme underlying community service work and collaborative group work is that all people inherently and fundamentally possess unique skills and traits that need to be identified and utilized for successful goal attainment.

Groups can only develop psychological cohesion by first identifying the various roles among each group member. While these roles may shift throughout the group process, it is critical that all members feel as though they have some important skill to contribute to the group itself. Cohesion is critical among all groups and can only develop when all group members are aware of their goal and use various skills in achieving that goal. Often individuals who have identified their unique skills can also express their identity and function within the group. A therapist, for example, may provide communication and cohesion within the group, whereas other group members may provide structure or leadership within the group. The unique and inherent value of any group is that it typically consists of several individuals with many diverse skills and aptitudes. Furthermore, individuals within the group can often display various skills and share these qualities with each other as goals become achieved.

When all members within the group are capable of applying their skills in a productive and useful manner, cohesion results and the goals of the group are achieved. More importantly, individual members within the group generally feel appreciated and are usually recognized for their effort by others. In a sense, then, each member feels that his or her unique skill played an important role in achieving the goal itself. When individual group members feel as though they have unique contributions to make to the group that results in an overall improvement to the group, individuals feel better about themselves (self-efficacy) and the group functions more dynamically (a phenomenon commonly referred to as *collective self-efficacy*).

Given the fact that the United States is a highly individualistic country that strongly supports autonomy and independence, it is important that we also teach children by way of comparison that collectivistic principles, such as cooperative group work and community service projects, are not the antithesis of autonomy and success, but rather actually complement improved group performance. Children are significantly more likely to incorporate and use the inherently valuable characteristics of group work if they are exposed to its benefits and application early on in development (Brewer & Brown, 1998). Conversely, if children are exposed to negative models that display traditional individualistic traits (i.e., egoistic and selfish behaviors and attitudes), then they are significantly more likely to incorporate these less desirable traits as well (Ma, Shek, Cheung, & Tam, 2002).

However, when children are exposed to the social and psychological benefits of community service and group work principles, they are motivated to begin future tasks within the group, and the overall productivity of the group exponentially increases when all members work cohesively. Community service work and cooperative group work are critical functions within the community that allow individuals and children to discover the value and dynamic power that we all share. Realizing that the achievement of goals is only possible through cooperation helps reduce social friction and improve communication among individuals who would normally lack contact with each other. This fundamental process of group development is the very glue which brings people together in community service work.

Group process begins usually at a very early age when young children (usually age five and beyond) begin to learn that other children have learned different skills that may be used in the process of achieving various goals. Children at this age are beginning to move away from the egocentric characteristic that many young children possess and are able to recognize the skills of other children within their own group. They can share ideas, toys, and complete several projects together. It is important to note that part of the value of community service work specifically among children is that community service work can help children to grow away from their own egocentrism and allow them to understand and appreciate other children from different cultures and backgrounds.

Children and Group Structure

In our culture, we strongly emphasize the importance of teaching children autonomy and independent skills. This emphasis usually begins early on in development (i.e., three, four or five years) in teaching children how to dress and feed themselves and so on. These skills are very important in helping children to learn a variety of tasks in educational, physical, social and interpersonal skills. However, perhaps a second area of concern in teaching children important skills in their development is not only in working by themselves autonomously, but rather in teaching children how to cooperate with others in collaborative group work. Being autonomous is not mutually exclusive with teaching children group skills and the importance in working with others, such as through sharing and cooperative work. Teaching children cooperative learning skills may be as simple as developing effective listening skills, rewarding them when they begin to share their ideas with others and can learn to incorporate other ideas with their own. Our own culture within the western hemisphere has strongly emphasized the value of independence and autonomy, and only recently has this emphasis on independence been identified as conflicting with the inherent value of collectivistic and group-oriented behaviors.

Research addressing how children interact with others from different ethnic and cultural backgrounds also suggests a that successful and dynamic group means more than just placing individuals from different ethnic groups together. Successful interethnic group interaction also requires individuals within the group to identify specific skills and encourage them to work together in achieving these superordinate goals (Stephen, 1987).

Suggested ages in beginning to teach children to work in groups may start as early as five, six or seven years of age. Any time children play or work in small groups the principles of collaborative group work may apply and, more importantly, be *discovered* among the children. As children develop and mature with other children it is especially important that they learn how to work with others, share their ideas, and contribute to an overall theme of the group. If children are not exposed to these types of learning environments early on in their developmental process, it becomes significantly more difficult for them to participate in group projects where they must incorporate the ideas and suggestions of others. The principles of collaborative groups essentially remain the same, regardless of the ages; however, the nature of the tasks obviously change based on the skills and aptitudes of each member of the group.

Our next important question to ask relative to the development of cooperative groups is how do the groups evolve during the process? Typically there are five stages of development when groups first develop: identifying each other, identifying the problem, identifying the roles of each member, brainstorming and identifying as many viable solutions to the problem as possible, and finally identifying when it is time to disband the group:

The Five "I's" of Group Process

1. Identifying each other in the group: Introductions
2. Identifying the problem: Why are we here?
3. Identifying roles: Who takes on specific responsibilities?
4. Identifying possible solutions: How do we solve the problem?
5. Identifying task completion: When is it time to disband? Members are recognized for completing responsibilities. Just like the relatives who stay longer than three days in your house, sometimes groups are reluctant in realizing that their purpose and function has come to a close.

Step #1: Identify Each Other

Introductions with each student should be made. Generally when students meet each other for the first time, individuals create positive first impressions. Only through time and experience can all student group members develop a strong and accurate understanding of each other. Since each student may be in a different class, introductions are necessary and students need some time to communicate and orient themselves with each other. Students and individuals who are faced with a particular assignment work most effectively when they know each other and have an opportunity in identifying their strengths and weakness. Humor is often a very good strategy in helping individuals feel more relaxed, especially in a situation where none of them are familiar with their task. Once we have become aware of other group members and have identified each person who belongs within the group, our ability to identify the problem and communicate various problem-solving strategies improves significantly.

Step #2: Identify the Problem

Once the introductions have been made and the students feels more comfortable with each other, they now need to identify what their tasks are and what they need to do. The students in the group have been given the assignment of planting a vegetable garden and have been provided with instructions and the materials. They now need to develop a process or method in understanding how to complete the project in the most efficient method. The problems include how the garden is supposed to be created, what types of vegetables should be planted and where, how to prepare the soil, and how to water. Now the students need to determine how to get started with creating a garden, and to do this they need to assign roles. After the problem of identifying what needs to be done is resolved, members now need to identify who will actually be doing what.

Step #3: Identify the Roles

Once the problems have been identified, the next important task for the group is in determining their roles in carrying out the tasks. This is a very important responsibility in collaborative group work, as a major underlying assumption is that all individuals have several basic skills and aptitudes that they may offer to the group. The key to successful collaborative group work is when all members feel as though they have important things to contribute to the group and when there are opportunities for them to actually contribute to the group. For example, in the gardening assignment, one individual may be assigned a shovel to dig fertilizer into the ground and to prepare the soil for the vegetables and flowers. Someone in the group who feels particularly capable of doing manual work may volunteer for this particular task, whereas someone who is more specialized in selecting specific plants and the physical location of the vegetables and flowers may offer to determine the arrangement of the plants, and so on.

Each member of the group should be encouraged to volunteer their skills as much as possible so the role assignment may develop with few problems. Individuals are significantly more likely to respond positively to each other when we know who the people are and roles and responsibilities that have been assigned. Chances are very good that even though the students have been attending the same school (and even the same class), they still may not know each other. Empirical research consistently supports the idea that children are more likely to interact with other children of different ethnic and economic background when they have been exposed to various activities encouraging dialogue and recreation with each other. Children who are placed in small groups often learn to share responsibilities and roles within group interaction and are therefore more likely to develop interpersonal skills with diverse groups as they mature and develop. There are many different roles that evolve during the formation and development of the group. Some sample roles include:

- The Group Leader: The group leaders are typically individuals who need to assert their authority and maintain control during the progress and development of the group. In social psychology they are typically referred to as a "type A" personality. Group leaders are typically very communicative and persuasive individuals who know how to work with different personality types and can be diplomatic in achieving their goals;
- Information Provider: The information provider typically refers to individuals who need to provide information relevant to the group and how the group progresses;
- The Negotiator: The negotiator typically refers to the individual who feels compelled to help solve problems that develop among the members of the group, or someone who simply feels compelled to find harmony within the group;
- The "Chip on the Shoulder" Member: The "chip on the shoulder" individual is who resents being in the group and typically retaliates against others by maintaining a very confrontational approach to others. They are the types who typically are looking for a good confrontation or fight in the group;
- The Detached Individual: The detached individual maintains a non-committed approach during the entire group process and projects an "I couldn't care less" attitude throughout the group process. These types are very destructive to any means of group progress and can actively promote apathy and deterioration within the group itself if it is not addressed quickly;
- The Provider Individual: The provider individual feels compelled to

give or provide things for other members of the group. These individuals are typically very nurturing, sensitive and very compatible with other members of the group;
- The Counselor: In many group situations, some individuals feel an inherent need to support and protect other group members during tense moments. "The Counselor" refers to those individuals who provide interpretive insight to common group problems and help other group members to communicate effectively within the group.

Step #4: Identify Possible Solutions

Perhaps the greatest single advantage to the group work is the number of possible solutions that are made available. The realization of various solutions in itself is very productive in reducing stress and anxiety that the group may be experiencing. There are many unique and inherent advantages to groups who are diverse in their composite and development. For every problem that exists, there also are several potential solutions to that problem that may be applied. Members within the group are vital in helping to identify and select the most effective problem solving strategy that exists. The more those individuals who are within the group can communicate effectively with each other, the greater the chances that the group can develop solutions to various problems. Each member within the group (because of their diverse backgrounds and experiences) can provide unique insight and perspectives to various problems. Our ability to identify solutions is only part of our task in-group process— engaging in and integrating the solutions to the problem is another matter that needs clarification. Brainstorming is one critical method whereby individual members within the group work collectively to identify a variety of different potential solutions. Support and encouragement throughout this process is critical to enable group members to continue providing constructive information.

Step #5: Identifying Task Completion

When is it time to leave the group? Often groups have just as much difficulty in disbanding as they do initially in forming the groups. Most groups develop with some specific task in mind, either to render a decision in a jury room, to engage in recreation or sports, or to identify personal growth and insight in a self-help group. Just as all groups develop for a specific task or purpose, those groups eventually must come to the realization that their mission has been either a success or failure and that the time to dissolve is at hand. Hopefully, members of the group will agree that some meaningful purpose has been developed and achieved and that each can come away from the experience a more developed individual.

Types of Groups and the "Gestalt Effect"

There is something innately dynamic and beneficial when groups of individuals come together for a common positive purpose. Communities with volunteers who build homes after a tragic earthquake, flood or tornado are often able to quickly "bounce back" economically because of the work that is shared by most community members. The positive effects are popular and contagious, as many community members mobilize resources to help others in times of tragedies and crisis. Research has shown that community service work allows societies to utilize the skills of all group members, thereby improving the relationships that these members have with each other. The positive and reciprocal impact of community service work and volunteer work is very strong, as those individuals who have been helped in the past are significantly more likely to help others in times of future crisis.

Groups of individuals (when organized and cohesive) are much more powerful and dynamic than collections of individuals. In competitive team sports, for example, teams can only win when all members work collectively. When outstanding athletes lack the ability to work as an actual member of a team, failure typically results regardless of how talented the individual may be. The founder of the Gestalt movement, Max Wertheimer, has argued that a key element in understanding human behavior was in viewing behavior from a collectivistic and holistic view. All humans are unique and different based on environmental and genetic variations, and in order to understand each person we need to consider all of these factors.

The Gestaltist phrase, "The whole is more than the sum of the parts," refers to the fact that each individual cannot be viewed separately or outside of his or her environment, but rather they should be viewed as a critical, unique and viable component to a dynamic society. Furthermore, the Gestaltists would agree with the fundamental philosophy of the community service work principles, where humans function best and most efficiently when we feel that we are a part of a group and that we are contributing to the group itself. Human antisocial behavior, such as aggression, hate crimes and gang behaviors begin when individuals feel as though they have nothing to offer the community and society, and that their community and society have nothing to offer them. They feel that it is impos-

The Gestalt Prototype

sible to belong to a culture or community that offers them nothing, so they create their own small "violent community" as a way of asserting their identity and purpose. Gangs have increased in popularity due to the lack of a community to provide individuals with a sense purpose and belonging, such as a family, so the gang becomes the artificial family to the individual. Crime is often the result of a community that lacks opportunity and education, as individuals become alienated from the community itself.

According to the fundamental Gestaltist theory, it is the responsibility of the community and society to help individuals discover their passion and skills in life through the context of group work. Educational institutions, such as colleges and universities and providing economic opportunities are the key mechanisms in helping people to identify their strengths so they will naturally feel to be an integral component of the group itself.

M. C. Escher's (1938)
Woodcut Relativity

The Gestaltist movement in psychology is critical to group dynamics and community service work principles because the combined efforts of group members is significantly more powerful than the individual strengths of those members. Participating in a community service project and virtually seeing the positive effects of a once-graffiti strewn community now flourishing with healthy and vibrant plants is extremely positive and motivating. Realizing that these goals could not have been achieved without the collective efforts within the group fully embodies and embraces the central philosophy of both Gestaltism and community service work: The end product (whole) is more than the sum of the individual—community service work is the cohesive group utilizing each member to achieve each goal.

Imagine seeing a rose for the first time and having someone ask you the difficult question: "In your opinion what makes a rose a beautiful plant?" There are many possible (and all accurate) responses. You may respond: "The color of the rose" or you may say: "The fragrance of the rose." But if you are like most people, you would respond: "Really a rose is beautiful because of the combination of several variables, such as fragrance, color, and so on." In many ways, the advantages of community service work are similar to the many characteristics of the rose.

Community service work is dynamic and powerful because of the combination of several characteristics of many different people, and it is impossible to limit your response to just a few comments. It really is the combination of numerous unique human characteristics and qualities that make community service work truly a dynamic and humanistic quality.

Why Do Groups Exist?

Different groups exist for different reasons. Some groups become established to help each other (i.e., support groups) whereas other groups exist for a common purpose (i.e., jury groups, troubleshooting groups, etc.). Most groups become established to serve some common cause or purpose and may specialize in identifying different types of solutions. Substance abuse groups help each other by not only providing support for each other, but they also continuously provide each other with suggestions to help with specific types of problems. There are four primary types of groups that we will discuss: self-help groups, support groups, direct help groups and at-risk groups (i.e., older populations).

Self-Help Groups: The Group Helps the Individual

In self-help groups, typically one individual experiencing some form of a problem receives help from the entire group. For example, an individual who is trying to recover from depression or domestic abuse may seek out assistance from other individuals who are recovering from similar disorders. Group members in self-help groups direct their input towards one individual with an emphasis in helping that one person. All members of the group are directing their efforts towards one person. Self-help groups are particularly effective when one person or individual is experiencing a specific problem and they need support from others who may also have experienced similar problems in the past. In these types of situations, the group members themselves actually become positive role models for the one individual who is afflicted with a particular issue or problem. The group support system operates under the principle of "If we can do it, then so can you."

Support Groups: The Individual Helps the Group

Conversely, in support groups, all persons meet regularly to help each other, relatively a reciprocal form of support. No single person becomes the focus of group interaction, but rather all group members exchange information relatively equally. A common theme among the support group is substance abuse.

Direct Groups

In direct help groups, usually one person (i.e., a therapist) directs the flow and direction of the therapeutic process and allows members to contribute their feelings throughout the group's exchange of information. Each type of group process has advantages and disadvantages, but the primary advantage of each group design is the fact that several individuals work together for a common cause and they focus on a common problem. The mere fact that several individuals volunteer their time to work out potential solutions for one person within the group is in itself *ipso facto* healing and dynamic. Similarly, research has also supported the theory that individuals often misunderstand the intentions of others outside their group and exaggerate perceived differences (Chambers, Baron, & Inman, 2006).

At-Risk Groups

A new form or type of group that has been quietly growing in rapid proportion is the at-risk group. Several categories of individuals may fall under the parameters of "at risk" however, we will include a group that has been growing at alarming rates and actually requires the attention of the community itself. The elderly homeless are now the fastest growing group within the community that requires assistance and has been described as being the most vulnerable. According to the most recent Los Angeles County estimates, the elderly have become the fastest growing homeless population, with numbers as high as 3,000 to 4,000 (total homeless estimates are over 65,000 persons) within Los Angeles County alone (*Los Angeles Times*, "L.A.'s Elderly Homeless Population is Growing," March 20, 2008). The problem is complex, with many of these individuals (over 62 percent) having been identified with some form of mental or psychological disability. The traditional at-risk groups require special attention from the community, where individuals need to work together to create some form of shelter and support for each homeless person.

Community service groups often combine the benefits of each of the three forms or types of groups. Community service work often helps individuals by promoting and increasing how they feel about themselves and their self-esteem. Community service groups also help agencies and organizations by improving them in some way, such as cleaning the litter in the area, planting flowers and improving the aesthetic appearance of the school, park or public institution. Finally, community service work also provides many benefits that are found in direct help groups. Community service activities not only serve to help improve the community itself, but can help individuals identify a common theme with the people they work with. Community service work helps to improve how we feel about ourselves and empowers us to take on new challenges. The group provides an effective process where we can identify our own skills through the combined efforts of others within the group. In this dynamic way, individuals not only feel more capable of taking on new responsibilities, but community service work has also been shown to be highly instrumental in helping individuals to discover new strengths and aptitudes for future challenges, things that they were not previously aware of.

4

The Dynamic Relationship between Collaborative Learning and Community Service Work

WORKING TOGETHER FOR A COMMON PURPOSE

When individuals work cooperatively in groups they are able to share and exchange information in such a way that their ability to problem-solve improves significantly. Moreover, the learning process typically is more dynamic and students report having "fun" during the learning process. All one needs to do to verify the claims of the effectiveness and enjoyment among members of group work is to personally observe this phenomenon in any classroom and see how the students or members relate and engage in interaction.

To collaborate, literally defined, means to share and exchange information in a supportive manner, where groups engage in a task to achieve a mutually beneficial goal. This purpose may be to complete an assignment in class or to improve a community recreational park. Recent research addressing interethnic and collaborative group work has shown that multiculturalism actually enhances creativity in educational and organizational environments (Leung, Maddux, Galinsky, & Chiu, 2008). Groups exist in many forms and may progress under many different circumstances. Individuals may form groups for fun and entertainment (i.e., organizing a bowling or softball team), business (i.e., organizing a task force to identify what product is most effective for a particular group) or to determine guilt or innocence of a defendant (i.e., a jury decision). A clear advantage to community service group work is simply in the potential efficiency in which it can work—combining the sheer talent and potential of several individuals in an organized and structured process inherently maximizes the power of the group's ability to achieve success in a variety of different problem situations that exist today. Additionally, a second advantage of group work is its vast popularity among students and the relative ease in the development of group work. Successful group work is also highly versatile and can be incorporated in a vast array of different types of learning and educational environments.

Community service work is an example of collaborative learning that is usually designed to improve a public environment (such as a school or recreational area). The learning process that typically occurs with collaborative learning is also evident in community service work. In community service work projects, individuals learn from two separate yet interrelated links— they typically learn from each other in their dialogue and exchanges with each other, and they typically learn about the project they are completing. For example, in the Compton Community College community service project, students not only learned about each other (i.e., reduced and debunked stereotypes among various ethnic groups), but they also learned about agricultural topics, such as planting citrus trees, vegetables, and flowers. Furthermore (and perhaps even more importantly), the students who were involved in the project brought their own children, so they too were exposed to the positive educational benefits of learning about people from different ethnic backgrounds and planting vegetables.

There are many different types of environments that may be used with collaborative learning, and collaborative learning skills are not just traditionally used in the educational disciplines or in the classroom. The concepts of collaborative learning transcend far beyond the classroom, where children and adults may benefit from collaborative group work in community service activities (i.e., cleaning up neighborhood parks, community colleges, or beaches), sports and recreation (teaching children basic concepts relative to sharing that are inherent in cooperative group work), and many other types of activities.

In this chapter we will explore the relationship between collaborative group work (typically seen in educational and professional institutions) and community service work. We will also explore how academic skills and performances may be increased when teachers incorporate the basic principles of collaborative and cooperative work. We will also compare the processes of collaborative group work with community service work and illustrate the similarities of each process. When individuals within the community join ranks and work together, incredible things can happen. When students within the classroom work cooperatively together on a mutual task, the educational experiences are also improved.

Collaborative Group Work
within the Classroom —
Learning as an Interactive Process

Part of the advantages of having technology in higher educational institutions is that students may learn to solve problems faster and more independently. With technology in the classrooms, students may use laptops to surf the net to find information in a fraction of the time that it took with traditional textbooks. Part of the problem, however, in incorporating the use of technology in classrooms is that students tend to become psychologically isolated from each other. Automated devices combined with technology, such as the internet, make information access much faster and easier. In the past, when students needed to review literature and cite important information for an important paper, they often worked together to save time and share ideas. Today, often many students feel as though group work and interaction with others is irrelevant, as the amount and intensity of work has become facilitated through technology. Additionally, frequent work that is conducted in isolation often gives the (incorrect) perception of autonomy without the benefit and use of those working with us in the same environment. Collaborative group work is especially ideal in bringing people together because it provides direct and first hand contact with our work partners. Working via email or the internet can often provide problems relative to communication as well as losing the context of the message due to actual physical distances involved in the work.

Consider the disturbing trend that is growing especially among younger people — purchasing electronic technologically related devices that claim to have the same benefits as engaging in group tasks with others. Video games, for example, are rapidly becoming the popular choice of recreation among many children primarily because of how advertisers sell the product. A video game that allows for "interactive" or "virtual" experiences sells the notion to the public that children can get the same benefits (physical as well as educational) by playing with these products. But is this really true? How can children learn from their experiences sitting in a room playing with an electronic device by themselves? How is learning, sharing, communicating, collaborating, or compromising achieved with a virtual interactive baseball game? Where are the physical benefits? As you can hopefully see, there are numerous disadvantages to children's physical and psychological development when they select interactive games that prevent them for developing the exclusive benefits that are associated with collaborative recreational play with other children.

Collaborative work simply means groups of individuals working together and sharing a common goal — this goal may be business related, such as a group of employees working towards a project, a group of jurors determining a verdict, or simply groups of individuals having fun and competing against each other in recreational activities. In this section of collaborative group work, we will discuss how team efforts really embody the concepts and advantages of collaborative group work. Additionally, a team means just that — a collection of individuals working as a single unit.

Children and Cooperative Groups

Up until now, we have been discussing the numerous benefits of community service work and cooperative group work relative to adults and college students. There is another population that is especially amenable to the benefits of group work and community service work and that would be children. There are numerous advantages to using collaborative group work with children. When children form groups to engage in recreation, they are afforded opportunities to learn from each other and engage in activities that help develop their physical and communicative skills. They can learn problem-solving abilities and communication skills when confrontations inevitably (and often) develop. They learn to engage in teamwork to work towards a common goal that establishes support and interdependency among one another. Children learn not only the value of working with others in collaborative groups, but they also learn key functions necessary for later development, such as delay of gratification in achieving goals, cooperation, and improvements in communication skills with those persons who may be different from them in some way. In short, they learn to trust and confide in each other that builds valuable skills as they mature — skills that are necessary in later interaction as adolescents and adults.

Teaching collaborative skills while playing sports and engaging in recreation is a very effective method for teaching children and adults the inherent advantages of team work and collaborative group work. Teaching children how to win as well as how to lose is also critical. Showing children what kinds of things they learned from their interactions with each other is a very valuable asset that focuses on the process and experience of the activity and removes the importance of "winning at all cost" attitudes. When children grow and learn in their relationships with each other in recreation and sport, they are really learning more about themselves and benefiting from these experiences with others.

Collaborative Group Work and Recreational Activities

There are actually many different types of activities, recreational or athletic, that lend themselves well to the concepts of collaborative group work. All team sports (at least in theory) embrace the concepts of group work by focusing on the talents of each player. Only when players work together (i.e., "are in the zone") can the team play at its best. The type of sport may vary from baseball to basketball to soccer. The important component regarding cooperative learning and recreation is that everyone feels as though they are contributing to the achievement of the goals of the group. The function and purpose of the group is to have fun, engage in healthy competition, and to learn the value of sportsmanship. The advantages of collaborative group efforts in recreational activities are where all members can play an instrumental role while competing and having fun. Invariably, some members may be more skilled and talented than other members. Have group members who are skilled in some areas teach their skills to other group members. Some key points to keep in mind when organizing collaborative skills in recreational activities:

• Make sure that all members of the group can identify their goals and their skills, and then place individuals where their skills match their position on the team;
• Try to encourage the more advanced members to work and to teach the less skilled members their tips in improved performance. Limit the group to four, six or eight members, depending on the nature of the sport that the group is engaging in;
• Have members on the team trade off in different positions so that they can change positions when necessary;
• Remind children to focus more on having fun and enjoying the experience of the activity rather than simply focusing on "winning";
• Have members review what their responsibilities; and
• Practice, practice and practice some more!

Collaborative Group Work and Education: Learning Can Be Fun When Working with Others!

The concept of collaborative group work in higher education is a very dynamic topic today. Today more than ever it is important that educators try to utilize the skills and knowledge that students have from difference backgrounds and cultures. One of the best ways in which students can learn critical information is by providing an environment where they may learn from each other. Collaborative (or sometimes referred to as cooperative) education is a unique and dynamic process of learning where students learn to rely and depend on each other's skills and aptitudes in creating the most comprehensive project available. Teachers who incorporate cooperative group assignments with other more traditional types of work assignments in their classes are truly affording their students the most efficient way to use information with other students.

Teachers in virtually any discipline can incorporate the benefits of cooperative group work into their class. Depending on the length and type of class lecture, teachers may first discuss the material to students in a traditional lecture and then break them up into groups of three of four. Teachers may then provide questions to the group based on the lecture material and, perhaps more importantly, the questions may be written in a manner that allows all members to contribute in answering the questions. Given the fact that psychology often has many different perspectives and points of views, questions may be phrased in such a way where groups may divide the question into four sections. For example:

Psychology is the science of behavior and mental processes. There have been many different theorists who have described behaviors among people in many different ways. In our discussion this evening, we have reviewed four basic theories in psychology: a) Freud's theory of psychoanalysis and the unconscious mind; b) Behavioral theory and operant conditioning; c) Cognitive theory and principles of learning; and finally d) Biological Psychology and how the brain influences behaviors. In your assignment you will be required to describe each basic theory of psychology and identify the strengths and weaknesses of each perspective. You will have thirty minutes to complete this assignment.

Students who are enrolled in a typical introductory psychology class may have several notes from different lectures and putting all of the information from the lectures together in a comprehensive and meaningful format can be very difficult. Different students may have different notes, and collaborative group work allows each student to show and compare their information and create a single assignment that is most comprehensive and thorough. Part of the advantages of collaborative group work is that the project that is being completed by each person can be used as a good summary tool that incorporates various theories in psychology together. For example, if the psychology project asks several questions— such as: a) Describe Freud's theory of psychoanalysis; b) Describe the scientific method and provide examples; c) Compare the Humanistic theory with the Psychoanalytic theory; and finally d) Identify the three parts of the brain (hindbrain, midbrain and forebrain)—these are all very comprehensive topics.

In collaborative group work, if the group consists of four individuals, each person can spend approximately fifteen minutes on each problem and then share their work with members and then revise each section based on group members' comments. During the actual group work, students may share ideas and collaborate with each other, or they may simply work individually for a short period of time and then show each other their work and critique their work. Perhaps the single most important benefit of collaborative group work among students completing academic assignments is that through this process each student is afforded the opportunity to present his or her own experiences and insight as a contribution in answering questions. Each member of the group first identifies how they will contribute to the problem and they then share their overall views. Information then becomes further processed until the final product actually becomes an amalgamation and synthesis of the group from each member.

Collaborative Group Work and Community Service Work: Improving a Community College via Gardening Activities

We have stated previously that one primary advantage to group and collaborative work is the versatility of the principles in a variety of situations and environments. Community service work and gardening are two activities that both work very well with the principles of improving interaction among ethnically diverse groups of individuals. How can groups who participate in a community service program such as gardening actually have changes in the levels of ethnocentrism? For the last several years, students at Compton Community College have been doing just that — working together collaboratively with other students from different levels of education and ethnicity that has resulted not only in improving the community college itself, but, more importantly, improving the levels of interaction among ethnically diverse groups within that community.

Planting a Vegetable Garden as a Group Activity: What Are the Advantages?

There are numerous advantages to the experiences of community gardening. Perhaps the most obvious advantages to gardening activities are that they are fun, healthful and educational experiences for individuals of all ages—children as well as adults (and older adults as well). When planning a garden, individuals can work together in terms of not only what types of vegetables or flowers to plant, but how they should be planted for optimum appearance and beauty. Gardening enhances not only physical health by being outdoors and doing lots of manual labor, but it can also enhance our psychological health by reducing stress and working in a creative environment. Gardening may also help people to discover their artistic and creative skills—for example, designing a small vegetable area by color or in a specific pattern is a very popular activity among gardening enthusiasts. Part of the psychological benefits of gardening also includes the fact that it provides an excellent environment that enhances and stimulates communication among individuals in a very relaxing environment.

Additionally, gardening activities can help teach children the value of respecting nature and ecology, as well as providing information addressing the importance of being environmentally responsible and protecting our environment. In this era of global warming and excessive carbon emissions, gardening helps as humans to get back to our roots, when our ancestors spent the majority of time simply in search of food and agricultural development.

How Is Gardening Done?

Gardening can either be an individual or a group task, and when groups of individuals work cooperatively on a mutually defined goal, the rewards can be very stimulating and rewarding. Our current gardening project is designed to improve a community college garden plot. The area that the students will be working in covers approximately one-half to one full acre, so there are many things to do. The primary benefits of any group task are when all persons feel as though that they can contribute towards a mutual goal. In this case, gardening requires:

1. A Digger: one or two people who can cultivate the soil with a shovel;
2. A Weeder: one or two people to remove weeds from the soil;
3. A Mixer: one or two people who mix the soil amendments in the dirt;
4. Planner: one or two people who plan the physical design of the garden — what gets planted and where it is located;
5. A Planter: individuals who actually plant the vegetables, flowers and trees in the correct locations; and finally
6. The Watering Person: individuals responsible for watering the plants.

Let's assume that we are working with a broad range of individuals — some of the students may actually be community college students, some may be high school students, and we may even have children from some of the community college students (ages five, six or eight years). A primary advantage of cooperative group work is that it is very effective regardless of the ages of the individuals who actually comprise the group. Cooperative group work can be just as effective in working with children as it is with older individuals nearing retirement age. The key factor to successful cooperative group work is in structuring the task so all members feel as though they are contributing to the task itself. Again, the key concept relative to successful groups and community work is achieving interdependency.

In the current project we provided groups of community college students (ages 18 through 30) with a variety of plants and vegetables. We also provided them with an open garden area to begin their work. The first goal of the project was in assigning roles — who was going to do what particular activity. Each group was provided with specific instructions in terms of how to get started, what to plant and so on. Each group working in the garden area was very diverse and reflected the demographics of Los Angeles, California. El Camino College — Compton Center is very diverse in terms of ethnicity and is located in an urban area that typically does not offer many opportunities where students can learn about planting vegetables. In this particular type of research situation involving cooperative work, the circumstances were ideal in the sense that all of the students were limited in their knowledge in planting vegetables and all had to work together to successfully create their garden.

The Value of Community Service Work: Changing Blighted Areas into Beautiful Gardens

The popularity of community gardens has risen significantly over the last decade. Communities need to provide people with the opportunities to work, play and interact with each other in an outdoor environment. As communities and neighborhoods become increasingly congested with and affected by housing and growth, there still remains a very basic and vital need for individuals within the community to contribute, improve and enhance their living environments through the development of community gardens. As neighborhoods become increasingly affected, there has been a trend in developing community gardens where public areas are now being transformed into beautiful gardens.

Numerous public agencies (i.e., Department of Water and Power, Flood Control District) have traditionally kept large parcels of land in gated areas, keeping the public out. These gated areas are usually very ugly from an aesthetic perspective — litter, weeds, abandoned cars, graffiti, sofas and many other types of debris litter the areas. Many "smart communities" are now taking advantage of the basic gardening need that many people have and are changing these previously vacant and ugly areas into very beautiful and well-kept gardens. More importantly, the relationship is reciprocal, where the community is being improved (for free) and citizens are able to work in the own creative "garden plot" (often with their children). For example, the Department of Water and Power, Bureau of Land Management, and even the Flood Control District are offering various parcels of land that are being transformed into beautiful garden areas. This is a very good example of how planning and sensitivity to the needs of members of the community can improve the overall landscape of the environment where people live. This is also a good opportunity to describe how gardening plots in previously vacant areas now provide people with an opportunity to help their community and also provide a sense of purpose (interdependency) for those persons who maintain the garden areas.

Environments that encourage members of the community to become proactively involved (such as gardening) are helping to prepare and teach young persons the tools necessary for successful professional development. Additionally, the benefits of community gardening can also help older adults to improve their quality of living, provide a sense of meaning and purpose in their daily responsibilities involving gardening. Finally, community gardens may also serve as a social base for older adults to make new friends who share similar interests.

The first step in establishing our community garden is in establishing roles—people need to know what they are responsible for. When people know what they need to do, the overall work process is very enjoyable. If you recall earlier in the chapter we discussed how groups begin their development through the "Five I's": identification of group members, identifying the problem, identifying the roles, identifying various possible solutions, and identifying when the group has accomplished its task and is ready to disband.

Once the roles have been determined and people know what to do, everyone should begin working. There are actually several ways in which groups can distribute work responsibility relative to the gardening task. The group members can either determine that all members of the group do all things, or members may actually shift roles during the group process. After several hours of cultivating, digging and mulching fertilizers in the soil, the group members can begin planting the flowers, vegetables, trees, and shrubs. Usually the most successful gardening experiences involve all group members sharing responsibilities and engaging in their work together.

For example, if the first task of gardening is in cultivating and mulching the soil, then all group members (n = 6) may begin work with shovels and begin weeding and cultivating the soil. Some of the benefits of gardening work are simply derived from the manual labor involved—digging and cultivating are two very strenuous activities even for a short period of time (i.e., 15 minutes). After the group has completed their first phase of the project, the next phase is in actually planting the materials. Some members of the group may wish to plant vegetables only, whereas others may wish to plant flowers and trees. All members should be provided with an opportunity to express their desires in the planting design and some agreement should be reached.

With most groups who work in community service gardens, the most rewarding component and satisfying aspect of the gardening work is in simply being outside and sharing in the physical and manual labor. All group members communicating their opinions usually determine how the garden is displayed and the majority of the group determines the decision. When individuals work cooperatively together, their relationships with each other improve significantly. Not only do the relationships among participants improve with each other, but past research shows that attitudes towards race, religion and gender have been shown to improve as well. Community group work, whether creating a garden or improving a neighborhood, has been shown to be a highly effective activity in bringing groups of people together.

5

The Relationship between Community Service Learning and Interdependency

OUR "EXTERNAL" DIFFERENCES HELP US TO REALIZE OUR "INTERNAL" SIMILARITIES

What is the nature of group interaction and communication? How can individuals who come from different backgrounds and cultural experiences engage in meaningful dialogue and discussion? For a diverse and lively discussion among any group of individuals, simply ask each person how they may best communicate with other people in different types of social or professional environments. Chances are very good that you will receive a wide range of responses. Some of the more "idealistic" individuals may respond that different groups are naturally predisposed to just "get along" with each other, whereas the more critical people may indicate conflict is always a factor to consider when dealing with different groups. The reality is, however, that different groups of individuals have always existed as long as people have existed. Furthermore, the existence of differences within each group has served a variety of purposes.

The key point to mention relative to this chapter is in recognizing and understanding that these perceived differences should be viewed as potential strengths relative to group development and is clearly within our power to improve if we truly wish to. Many sociobiologists and evolutionary psychologists have argued that early group formation and cooperative behaviors were critical to our survival as a species. Thus, the ability to engage in cooperative and collaborative group work, especially when it is designed to improve our reproductive fitness, is something that is innate and inherent within our chemistry. Whether or not we wish to "fine tune" and rediscover these necessary genetic predispositions lies entirely up to us in social and community development programs, such as community service work.

Our differences among groups served to help us to develop adaptive skills throughout our evolutionary history. These primary differences among people have always served as both inherent advantages relative to our very survival and the source of conflict and disadvantages relative to human interaction (Hill, 2003). A primary focus of this text is in showing the reader how differences among individual members of the dominant group can serve inherently as advantages to our daily functioning in society.

In the earliest examples described by sociobiologists and evolutionary theorists (Wilson, 1972), the formation of groups (or clans) helped to protect people from various types of threats in their environment. Some of these threats were from natural predators and some were even from other nearby clans or groups of individuals. There were clear advantages to those individuals who congregated and lived in small groups—food was easier to come by and having several people nearby meant having more resources to help one exist and survive during difficult times. Quite ironically there were also benefits to those groups of people or clans that tended to congregate among each other that were phenotypically (i.e., outward characteristically) similar in appearance. Interaction or complacency with "different" groups of people from different environments (i.e., strangers) other than the dominant group often resulted in fatal consequences (Gould, 1996).

Clearly, then, an adaptive mechanism was formed through evolution where individuals avoided direct contact or interaction from others who were somehow phenotypically different from themselves. This may explain in some cases why members of different ethnic groups have experienced hostility and outright rejection from their efforts to assimilate to the dominant group. Additionally, the evolutionary characteristic may account for what many social psychologists refer to as the "negativity bias." The negativity bias simply claims that individuals show more attention and concern towards potentially harmful events that can pose a hazard to our own safety.

In an interesting study that underscores the negativity bias, Ohman, Lundqvist, and Esteves (2001) conducted an experiment that showed subjects a variety of faces with different expressions, some happy, some angry, and some neutral expressions. The researchers discovered that the subjects were significantly more likely to recall the negative facial expressions that were identified as being anger or aggression. Thus, humans have an uncanny ability to identify and sort out potentially destructive situations or unfamiliar faces that may pose as a threat to our safety. Relative to our own evolutionary history, we can assume that attending to anything that may have been threatening to our safety and group cohesiveness was clearly an adaptive survival mechanism. We can also conclude that strangers having unfamiliar faces most likely triggered a negative response that probably served as both an important safety and adaptive mechanism long ago that aided our own survival.

Getting to Know Strangers: Overcoming Negativity Bias

While it may be true that humans have evolved with an innate predisposition to be wary of strangers with unfamiliar faces (Izard, 1991), it is also true that humans developed a unique capacity to cooperate with each other by sharing skills and commodities. In an interesting study conducted at the Max Planck Institute for Evolutionary Anthropology, researcher Keith Jensen discovered that when chimps were placed in a food-sharing situation, chimps were most likely to maximize their own condition by taking all of the food and leaving no food available for the chimp's partner. What caught Jensen's attention, however, was not the fact that the chimps took any and all food available for themselves, but rather the response of the other chimp. The remaining chimp that was left without any food simply showed no signs of frustration or aggression: "It makes perfect economic sense to accept any nonzero offer and to offer the smallest amount possible while keeping all of the raisins for yourself" (*Los Angeles Times*, "A Sense of Fair Play is Only Human," October 7, 2007).

Conversely, humans have evolved with some sense of fairness. Without some notion of justice or fair play, cooperative or collaborative behaviors would be most unlikely, and without reciprocally cooperative behaviors among kinships, survival would have been virtually impossible. Thus, we can see the key evolutionary dynamics that justify unique human behaviors, such as justice, empathy and even altruism as having key evolutionary backgrounds. This concept of fair play as being a critical element to human cooperation is very similar to what Robert Trivers (1971) refers to as "reciprocal altruism," A unique human trait where humans are significantly more likely to reciprocate cooperation, altruism, justice and even kindness if these behaviors are first directed towards us.

Environments that promoted cooperative and collaborative behaviors were more likely to facilitate the survival of all people simply because each group began to organize and pool their resources. The more that people worked together and shared individual responsibilities with each other, the more likely they would benefit from each other. Perhaps more importantly, as people benefited from each other, their future experiences and interactions became more positive, which involved greater reliance on each other. Groups gradually came to engage in a form of positive dependence where skills and traits were shared among each other, thereby creating a sense of need with each other that we refer to as interdependency. When groups of individuals exist and engage in helping behaviors with each other, the greater the likelihood that the group itself would thrive under a variety of negative or even dangerous conditions. The existence of small groups during our evolutionary history and development has now created a need among modern humans to still form and establish ties to groups in our society or community. Observe the most productive and resourceful communities and you soon discover a common theme where these environments utilize the skills and aptitudes among all of the inhabitants within that community.

Interdependency and Group Relations

A key component relative to the success of groups is that of *interdependence*. Interdependence refers to a phenomenon where groups of individuals share a common interest in achieving goals relative to their welfare and survival. Interdependence is commonly referred to as the "glue" that binds individuals together and makes groups unique and distinct from one another. Interdependence is the very fabric that helps bind communities together by graphically illustrating that individuals need each other (especially in times of crisis) and are exponentially more powerful by combining or pooling their skills within the group. When people realize that other members within the community possess skills to help maintain the group integrity, then their relationships become reciprocal and positive in nature. Interdependency also identifies the strengths and skills that individuals bring to the group, thereby making the overall group stronger, with more integrity.

While groups (by definition) are simply collections of individuals, they are *de facto* significantly much more than that. Groups are exponentially capable of producing much more when the actual group members work cooperatively with each other. For example, the famous psychologist and ethologist Kurt Lewin (1951) argued in his field theory that the behaviors of individuals within groups are a function of the aspects of the person as well as the environment: $B = f(P, E)$. Relative to the interesting concept of Lewin's field theory is that of Gestalt psychology. The Gestalt theorists argued that some elements (such as human consciousness) cannot be broken down into simpler units. This dynamic theory argues that groups are inherently more capable of becoming productive when the individuals comprising the group work (i.e., the person) work cooperatively with other members of the group (i.e., the environment). Progress (and more importantly *perceptions* of progress among group members) becomes exponentially stronger when individuals work collaboratively together, a phenomenon some social scientists refer to as *collective self-efficacy*. The Gestalt theorists also argued that individuals are unique creatures given their individual experiences and that in order to truly understand people and their behaviors, we need to consider them collectively within their environment. Trying to understand human behaviors by separating individual experiences is impossible, just as it is impossible in trying to separate the colors of a sunset or the colors of rainbow.

Gestalt Psychology and Group Cohesion

Long ago when the early modern branches of psychology began making their marks in science, an individual by the name of Max Wertheimer began making new discoveries to the power of groups and how groups influence individual behaviors and perception. A branch of psychology originally introduced in Germany in the early eighteenth century (now referred to as Gestalt psychology) postulated that human consciousness and behaviors can become significantly influenced in terms of how we view them. When we view things in their entirety or wholeness, we can often get an entirely different perspective as opposed to viewing things when they are in separate form. Sometimes, for example, when we break things down into their simple elements, they can profoundly lose their impact or meaning. Imagine, for example, you view a beautiful flower or rose on a spring day. What are the actual elements that make up the beauty of the rose itself? Can they be broken down or taken apart? Yes, they can be reduced to simpler elements, but when we do this, the meaning and experience relative to the stimulus is lost. A rose loses its beauty when we pull apart the petals and remove its beautiful fragrance. So is the case with understanding human behaviors, groups and the cultures from which people live in. When you remove the individual from his or her group or cultural identity, you lose sight of who that person truly is and you cannot accurately understand (nor appreciate) their truly unique human behaviors.

Relative to our discussion addressing the topics of ethnicity and group relations, Gestalt psychology is an important branch of psychology that explores the critical value of the entire cultural and interpersonal component in understanding the "true personality" of each individual. Breaking up the personality into separate components by separating the biological inheritance factors with environmental influences does not provide us with an accurate perspective of the personality. Just as the traditional Gestaltist Max Wertheimer indicated that when we break things into individual units they lose their meaning, the Gestaltist view argues that human behaviors must be looked at comprehensively (i.e., within the emotional, spiritual and cultural context) to truly and most accurately understand the individual human dynamic. The value and multiple benefits of community service work are largely based on the unique benefits and phenomenon of Gestalt psychology — where the "whole" (in this case, the community or the group itself) is more than the individuals who actually comprise the group. *The strength of the group in community service work is based on the combination of unique skills and talents of each person comprising the group, where a major assumption or tenet of community service work is that each person,* ipso facto, *contains skills and potential that are unique and applicable within the group.* The more individuals feel as though they are contributing to a group effort that actively utilizes these skills, the more compatible and effective the group becomes in achieving community-oriented goals.

Within group dynamics we see how unique individual behaviors develop because of the formation of the group itself, and how this process of human development can only exist within the framework of the group. A collection of five individuals within the group becomes inherently more dynamic because five individuals have now taken on a single group identity. Humans are in fact truly unique and dynamic creatures because all of their experiences and activities are literally combined into one element within the group dynamic. Thus, the "whole is more than the sum" simply refers to the fact that in order to truly understand our behaviors and consciousness, we need to evaluate all experiences as one entity. As with individuals, groups themselves are unique and can take on interesting characteristics. Groups may evolve from one phase (not knowing the roles of each member) to other, more advanced phases where the identity of several individuals changes into one collective identity capable of achieving and accomplishing much more as a unit.

In other cases, individuals have created groups as literal think tanks to establish the laws and legal foundations of society (such as our Constitution), or still other groups are formulated for recreational activities and enjoyment. Groups serve many important functions in many ways, and how we shape and create them not only influences individual behaviors within the group, but can also shape the way a community functions.

Groups take on many important characteristics throughout their development. Understanding the group is significantly different than understanding the separate individuals who comprise the group itself. Groups change and evolve as their individual members move in various stages of development. Group members interact with each other based on the task that faces the group. How group members relate to each other also depends on the roles of each individual: There are aggressor roles, harmonizer roles, communicator roles, and so on. Often within the group, during the beginning stages, conflicts may develop among group members. When individual members within the group lack trust with each other, there is a significantly higher likelihood of conflict developing in that group as well as disproportionate communication, both of which reduce the overall integrity of the group.

When individuals believe that members of other groups in society are similar to each other (i.e., "they are all alike") and that our own in-group members are more diverse, then out-group homogeneity bias develops. How group dynamics can influence cross-cultural psychology is a critical issue and relative to the out-group homogeneity theory. Group members tend to follow a specific process of development and share certain goals. The group takes on an identity and evolves from various stages, from identifying each role for each member to solving various tasks. When individuals from ethnically different groups merge together to form one group, their styles of thinking usually change as well as their individual identity. The "group identity" now changes the individual identity and this change of identity is what gives the group the maximum amount of potential for creative problem-solving skills.

The benefit of cultural and ethnic diversity within the group dynamic is that each individual who represents various ethnic identities may bring with him or her issues and problems that represent that specific culture.

In a sense, then, multiethnic groups become microcosms of the larger community and may present an ideal atmosphere that promotes the development of problem-solving strategies. Multiethnic groups can help improve our understanding of the problems that face our communities and larger societies by representing each problem by individual members. Each person within the group represents the problems that are associated with each cultural or ethnic group and expresses those concerns to the other group members. In this way key issues and problems are communicated to the other members and problem-solving strategies may develop in an open forum.

How Can Multicultural Groups Facilitate Change?

- Multicultural groups provide an opportunity of communication via social, economic and educational comparisons with other groups;
- Multicultural group members are capable of learning from one another;
- Multicultural group members promote change via feedback and learning; vicariously from one another, such as role playing and experiencing the problems of each group member;
- Multicultural groups can provide information to other group members about the history and culture of various minority groups comprising the dominant group that will facilitate communication and understanding among all group members;
- Multicultural groups can often effect change to the dominant groups via social influence and consistency in adhering to cultural attributes shared by all members of the group.

Multicultural Groups Provide an Opportunity of Communication via Social, Economic and Educational Comparisons with Other Groups

When individuals shape and form groups that are representative of different cultures within society, a dynamic opportunity for change exists. The individual members who represent the diverse groups within the community are afforded the opportunity to communicate key issues that impact the welfare and development of their own culture and ethnicity.

Key issues such as education, employment, and health are often the most common topics that are discussed and all members provide vital information and feedback to the group. Often during these group sessions information is presented in such a way that myths and stereotypes are debunked — and the key issue is that when each stereotype is replaced by accurate knowledge, our understanding of each other becomes significantly enhanced.

What are some of the key characteristics in which the small minority group may effect change in the larger group? Moscovici (1985) identified three key factors necessary in small group dynamics to effect positive change:

(a) Consistency: Members of the minority group must appear *consistent* in their opposition to the majority group opinions. For example, in the famous Brown versus the Topeka Board of Education (U. S. Supreme Court ruling, 1954), the vast majority of Americans were actually in favor of the "separate but equal" ruling that addressed how students were educated in public schools. However, civil rights groups and leaders of the community were solidified in their belief that separatist views were inherently unequal, and were eventually able to influence the court's overruling of this law. More recently we see a very strong minority group addressing the legality of current rulings that ban same-sex marriages. Perhaps in time the small (but growing) minority group who oppose this law may have similar results as the Brown versus Topeka Board of Education;

(b) Flexibility: A second key factor for minority groups to effect change in the larger society is to not appear rigid and unyielding in their stance and belief systems. Flexibility, communication and a willingness to compromise are key concepts leading to positive growth and allows smaller minority groups to make gradual changes in the dominant society; and finally

(c) Social Climate: The social context in which change is proposed is vital to whether or not the minority group is successful is effecting change to the dominant group. For example, in a very conservative political climate it may be very unlikely that a highly progressive or liberal initiative may be approved.

Attribution Theory and Interethnic Relationships

Understanding how group members resolve various types of problems and identifying what types of issues they feel that they ultimately have control over are critical issues that influence group cohesiveness. Increases in communication among each member within the group leads to an increased understanding of the causal attribution of behaviors (i.e., attribution theory—do members have control over the outcome of their situations?), which ultimately leads to increased capacity of positive change (see figure below):

When individual group members effectively understand the issues that are surrounding ethnic minority groups, their perception and willingness to help others improves significantly. For example, a common misunderstanding addressing multiethnic populations addresses the topic of attribution theory. Numerous research studies suggest that when individuals are perceived to be responsible for their own problems, the public is generally less willing to intervene and help (Weiner, 1985). Attribution theory is relative to theories of motivation in explaining how people address and resolve problems in their lives. In other words, attribution theory explains whether or not we perceive individuals should be responsible for their own behaviors because it explains the motives of their behaviors. For example, if the group of individuals were jurors in determining the fate of an individual who has been convicted of drunk driving several times, typically the group considers whether or not the individual should be held responsible for his or her actions. Thus, individuals in the group who perceive obesity, substance abuse or pedophilia as conditions that are biological in nature, then they are less likely to be held accountable for their actions because it is believed that it is "not their fault."

HOW CHANGE OCCURS
IN GROUP DYNAMICS

Step 1: Increases in Communication within
the Group — What Are the Problems?

↓

Step 2: Increases in Understanding of
Behaviors within the Group

↓

Step 3: Changes in Attribution
(Is the Individual Responsible for
His or Her Condition?)

↓

Step 4: Changes in Public
Attitude and Behavior

In Weiner's (1985) classic attribution research, three key factors were identified as critical features in understanding motives and behavior. The first key factor was controllability/uncontrollability, the second key variable was stability/instability, and the third factor was internal/external. How controllable were the events leading to the specific behavior in question? Individuals do have control over many facets relative to their personality, such as temper, responsibility, and so forth. If an individual is perceived as being a victim for circumstances outside of his or her responsibility (external factors) and this event occurred in an uncontrollable situation, the victim is perceived as not being responsible for the outcome of his or her behaviors. For example, if a person is late for work because their car breaks down, we typically do not hold them responsible (assuming that this does not happen too often). Conversely, if a person is late for work because they have overslept, we typically would hold them accountable for being late for work because this is something they have more control over.

An individual may control his or her consumption of alcohol or eating, for example, but if this condition is described as a genetic predisposition to a disease then we tend to hold him or her less responsible for abusing alcohol or becoming obese. If we perceive conditions as being stable and internal, we hold individuals responsible for their behaviors. If conditions are perceived as being unstable and external, then we are more likely to view them as victims of circumstances. Research strongly supports the idea that the public generally evaluates these three conditions as a means of determining personal responsibility, innocence and guilt. In understanding group behaviors and group dynamics, we also take into consideration these three key variables when determining personal control or responsibility over a variety of behaviors (Graham, Weiner & Zucker, 1997).

Conversely, if the group is convinced that the individual should be held accountable for his or her actions and more importantly that they in fact have control of their own destiny (i.e., disputing the psychological premise of genetically predisposed behaviors), the sentence more likely will be harsher. Thus how the group determines guilt or innocence is more dependent on how the group perceives the attribution of the individual and if it believes he or she actually maintains control over their own behaviors. Given the current climate of our culture and community, more and more individuals believe that they in fact have less control over their behaviors, perhaps as a condition to hold them less responsible for negative outcomes of those behaviors.

When the group can understand how individuals interact and behave in a variety of situations and can attribute causality (internal versus external), then individual behaviors can become either criticized by the group or supported. For example, if group members feel that discrimination and prejudice have been the dominant features that have repressed members of a minority group, then the dominant group is significantly more likely to engage in positive forms of change to assist the minority group.

Perhaps more than any other time in our history of cultural and social development, people need to develop the skills of mutual understanding and cooperation when living and working together. The thrust and main focus of our text has been designed to illustrate the value and necessity of community service work as a critical function of groups and how to improve relationships among ethnically diverse groups. The need to engage in community work is central and inherent in each individual, and when different groups of individuals share their skills with each other, our relationships improve significantly.

In this chapter we have reviewed fundamental theories relative to group performance and how our evolutionary history has enabled groups to enhance our survival as a species. The theories of negativity bias and Gestalt psychology theory are two clear examples where our survival as a species depended on group solidarity and collaboration. Perhaps our initial reluctance to form groups with people who we perceive as being fundamentally "different" from us may come from a very basic and primitive evolutionary trait such as the negativity bias. However, once groups are capable of development, regardless how fundamentally different they may appear in the early stages of group process, the Gestalt theory argues that our perceptions of individuals as well as the strength of the group itself becomes significantly more powerful and adaptive. This basic and fundamental evolutionary concept perhaps is most relevant in various types of community service work. Additionally, because the dynamics of the group change once individuals within the community work cohesively together, then traditional race-related problems (such as ethnocentrism and hate crimes) have been shown to significantly reduce. The benefits of community service work and collaborative group work are especially significant given the trend for societies and communities to become more ethnically and culturally diverse.

6

Community Service Work

IMPROVING COMMUNICATION AND
REDUCING STUDENT ETHNOCENTRISM

One of the most primary features of this text is in improving how members of different ethnic groups learn to interact, work and create dialogue with each other. A very important component among ethnically diverse communities is that they remain diverse but also engage in programs and activities that encourage interaction and assimilation. We feel that communities can clearly maintain their own cultural identity and still promote effective interaction among ethnically diverse groups. A key component to successful and productive diverse communities is through the philosophy and behaviors that promote their own cultural experiences and are embraced by all members within the community. Diversity in this regard is then regarded as an inherent strength that makes each community more adaptive and reflects different cultural values from each ethnic group.

A disturbing trend that is becoming more apparent within societies and communities is the tendency for younger cohorts and populations to engage in ethnic polarization or segregation based on ethnicity. Just visit most high schools or groups of people as they meet each other for the first time, and there appears to be very basic drives for people to congregate with those that most close resemble each other. Hispanic students tend to initially interact with other Hispanic students, African American students with other African American students, and so on. High schools, athletic teams, recreational activities and any other group that comprises a community should embrace the positive psychosocial and educational benefits of ethnic diversity through community service engagement. It is critical that we implement programs and activities that address interactive and interethnic skills among the group, as these activities promote diversity. Just as any other important skill needs to be learned and developed early

80

on in childhood development, those communities that teach the value of ethnic diversity and promote activities that engage in this philosophy are less likely to experience hate crimes and ethnocentrism. When individuals experience similarities with each other through cooperative group work and community service work, they are more likely to contribute to the benefit of others and engage in prosocial behaviors (Burnstein, Crandall, & Kitayama, 1994).

A very powerful component of community service work is not only improving the society or community in which we live, but also in improving *how* are relationships become structured with each other and how we perceive each other relative to ethnicity. A stubborn component of prejudice is the erroneous belief that people who appear to be physically different from us are different in many other ways. This is typically not true, but unfortunately has become a continuing theme in discrimination. An important component of the community service program, if not one of the most critical features, is the phenomenon of reduced ethnocentrism throughout the course of the project. Perhaps the most critical question to ask and the most dynamic effect of the community service gardening program developed from the context of the relationships between the mentors and the community college students.

An empirical study was conducted at the beginning of the spring 2007 semester involving students from three different tiers of education. The first group of students was community college students at El Camino College. These students were enrolled in a variety of psychology courses and were ethnically diverse, with ethnic groups ranging from African American (40 percent), Hispanic (50 percent) and Caucasian (10 percent) students. The second group of students consisted of four-year upper division students (mentors) who were enrolled at California State University Northridge (CSUN) and Pepperdine University and were earning independent studies credits through their participation. The final group of students consisted of graduate students who were enrolled at Pepperdine University in a master's level psychology course.

We hypothesized that all three groups of students who interacted with each other and established positive working relationships with each other in the community service garden over a period of one academic semester would score significantly lower in reports of ethnocentrism and show higher scores in the reports of the value of community service work and volunteer service. The mentors worked very closely with the community college students at Compton Community College. During this period of time, positive relationships emerged where both groups of students were afforded the opportunity to help each other. The mentors helped the community college students to not only improve the physical environment of the campus by participating in the gardening program, but more importantly, to develop a positive bond of trust where the CSUN and Pepperdine University mentors could identify with individuals who initially they had little in common with. The mentors discovered the value of community service work and formed positive friendships among the community college students, and the community college students were able to work and improve the campus environment and establish valuable bonds of friendships with the CSUN mentors.

Additionally, the CSUN and Pepperdine University mentors were able to assist many of the community college students in successful transfer to higher education as well as help with improvements in academic performance in psychology. The relationships between both groups of students was clearly a "win-win" situation, where both groups reported to have experienced very positive relationships with each other and to have grown intrinsically from these experiences. Our empirical results strongly support the hypothesis that community service work reduces ethnocentrism as well as improves perceptions of the importance of volunteer work: An independent samples t-test was conducted, with the following results: (2.95), $t(10) = -12.70$ ($p < .0001$).

These results strongly confirm the hypothesis that ethnocentrism can be effectively reduced by implementing a variety community service programs among ethnically groups of students attending community college. Additionally, in a self-entitlement culture such as ours where individualistic ideologies are valued tremendously over collectivistic philosophy, it is more important than ever to teach and encourage members of the community to work cooperatively together. Communities benefit through volunteer work and community service work by the numerous positive activities that are conducted in the programs, such as cleaning parks and beaches, planting flowers and trees in urban areas, and cleaning blight and graffiti within lower socioeconomic areas. Most importantly, however, we discovered that teaching individuals the value and benefits of the positive effects of community service work was an essential component of the program. Community service work, reports of positive levels of self-esteem and self-efficacy, and people "feeling better — both physically and mentally" were just some of the common comments and reports that they made during the community service project.

Another benefit of the community service program was that people learned that feeling good about themselves through helping others was something that they could individually control and teach to their children. Perhaps now, more than ever, children and young persons need to appreciate the value of community service work and the intrinsic rewards in helping others by engaging in the activities and being provided with the opportunities to learn first-hand what giving can mean to others who are less fortunate. The important activities that both the community college students as well as the mentors participated in was a community service program that allowed different groups of individuals based on economic class, ethnicity, religion and gender to come together and work cooperatively on a project that was designed to help improve a community college. As the groups of students and mentors progressively spent more time together and they could see that their efforts were producing something of value that would have been virtually impossible to achieve by themselves, their attitudes became more positive towards each other as well as the community service program itself.

It is regrettable and disheartening that many individuals who have been reared in a highly individualistic society such as ours may not realize the value and benefits of a cooperative program such as community service work. The benefits of individuals working cooperatively in community service work are significant, with more effort among individuals taking responsibility in making small but powerful steps to do their part to make their communities and neighborhoods safer, aesthetically pleasing to see, and more education-friendly. The consequences of an individualistic community are many, but perhaps the most damaging component of such as egoistic community is that people essentially act by and for themselves, with little regard for the welfare of others or the physical structure of the community itself. It should not be surprising to see more crimes involving corporate greed (i.e., Enron and Kenneth Lay) where individuals maximize their gains at the cost of others' welfare (i.e., pensions and retirement funds).

We have in fact created a culture of what we refer to as "self-entitlement" where the expectation and norm is in what others can do for you as opposed to what sacrifices you can make for the community. These types of cultures have difficulty in understanding the value and purpose of community service cited in the current study. This self-entitlement philosophy has become fostered and nurtured from the individualistic culture that we now live in. The initial reaction and response from these individuals is "You are doing all of this work and not being paid for it?" "You are giving up your Saturdays to pull weeds for nothing!" or "What do I get out of this?" It is very important to identify how valuable community service work is to all people because of the changes in self-empowerment and improving the community.

When individuals realize that they have an intuitive responsibility not only to themselves but also to the community in which they live, their attitudes in engaging in community service work and volunteer work changes from one of obligation to that of a willing participant. The students in the current community service program were so positively influenced by the overall value and benefits of a community gardening program that many still volunteer today without receiving any credits towards their degree. When asked why they are continuing their work, one former mentor indicated: "It is something that you have to experience personally, and for me, the positive feeling that I get in working with other students and improving the community is something that just goes beyond words.... I think that all students [especially high school students] should have the opportunity to participate in this kind of program."

Indeed, perhaps the most effective strategy in reversing the negative consequences of the self-entitlement and individualistic culture is in simply organizing more opportunities for these persons to participate in and experience (first hand) the overwhelming values and sense of tremendous personal satisfaction in giving and contributing towards the community service project such as gardening. Perhaps more importantly, when the mentors were able to show the community college students by way of example how volunteer work and community service work play such an important role in not only improving the infrastructure of a community but also how much better people responded and interacted in the process, the family members of the community college students, neighbors within the community and friends also participated creating a truly communial and prosocial interactive experience.

Styles of Communication, Community Service Work and Information Overload

A second component of research involving community service work is in observing how individuals actually communicate with each other while performing the work. An important component within successful community service projects lies within the communication process itself; how members communicate with each other often determines the success (or failure) of the community service project or program. When groups engage in active and direct communication with each other, information becomes more accurately and efficiently disseminated within the group and more importantly helps to improve working relationships among group members.

Modern Technology and Information Overload: Too Much of a Good Thing?

Modern technology is critical in helping people function and exist on a daily basis. Without technology, our means of communication (i.e., cell phones and email), transportation (automobiles) and many other functions in life would be severely limited. It is common for many people to now feel dependent on things that have been originally designed to facilitate their lives as a means of convenience. Unfortunately, many individuals have become entirely dependent on technological devices that are compromising the quality and context of our interpersonal relationships with others. The cell phone, car and personal computer have now become products that we use *in place or in lieu of* people, and many individuals are losing sight of the importance of interpersonal and direct human interaction that community service work inherently represents.

Much of the technology that we take for granted is compromising and deteriorating our relationships with people and, ironically, our quality of living in society. Modern technology used within the group that is not directly related to the project goal often becomes disruptive and distracting among group members, thereby reducing positive interactive skills and communication among group members. For example, cell phones may disrupt assignments and take individual group members from the focus of the task being completed. Motorists who use cell phones while driving not only jeopardize the safety of all drivers due to divided consciousness consequences, they cost all drivers more time on the road, as much as fifteen minutes (*The Daily News*, January 20, 2008). Additionally, it is very common for resentment to build among other members to see one group member frequently drawn from the group by excessive phone calls. Similar to an individual who is addicted to an illicit substance, the chronic cell phone user feels vulnerable when they are not within reach of their cell phone. This chronic need to have constant access to technological devices is referred to as "technological overload"—the need to be using some form of a technological device that interferes with the ability to establish and maintain direct relationships with others.

Imagine the last time that you attempted to work with another person who was engaged in a conversation on a cell phone or iPod. You needed their attention but they continued to talk on their cell phone, gesturing that they would be "just one more minute." What was your reaction? If you are like most individuals, you were probably frustrated that you were unable to complete your work because of the distractions caused by the cell phone as well as your co-worker's insensitivity to you.

In a study that attempted to empirically validate the negative consequences of chronic dependency on technological devices, Hoffman and Wallach (2006) conducted a study that explored the benefits of a community service gardening project that excluded the use of any technological devices, such as cell phones, iPods, or text messaging devices. In the study, the researchers identified a group of community college undergraduate students who frequently used cell phones and related devices and indicated that they preferred these devices over actual interpersonal interaction (measured on a self-report questionnaire). The researchers then created cooperative groups to begin a community gardening project that required direct and interpersonal interaction with other students. Additionally, the experimenters required that the students leave all of the technological devices at home and not use them during the course of the experiment. After six months of participation in the community service project, the students in the experimental group indicated that they now preferred direct interaction with other students and, more importantly, *that their perceptions of the importance of the use of cell phones significantly decreased.* The students who participated in the study also indicated that they felt they had "rediscovered the importance of really talking to people and working together," which was only made possible through the community service activity.

Ultimately it is people of the community that work together in achieving important goals that will benefit the members within that community, and all people have positive skills that they need to contribute in the effort to achieve these goals. Machines and technology may *help* us to achieve these goals, but machines can never replace the unique qualities and aptitudes that all people possess. People who work cooperatively together and pool their resources have historically been the groups most likely to survive and create a positive and supportive environment for each other.

Alfred Adler once was quoted: "No individual is ever more destitute or hopeless than the one who knows not how to share or contribute to the welfare of others." It was his positive view of human nature and belief that all people are driven through social interest to work together that first created the rift and conflict with Freud. Perhaps now, more than ever, is the appropriate time to teach others and experience ourselves the value and benefits in community service work as a means of better understanding not only those who live with us within our communities, but ourselves as well.

7

Community Service Work, Individualistic and Collectivistic Cultures

TEACHING PRINCIPLES OF GROUP DEVELOPMENT VERSUS INDIVIDUAL GAIN

Today our culture emphasizes more than ever the importance of *individual* success, *individual* achievement, *self*-recognition, autonomy and independence. The current philosophy within the individualistic culture is that the more that we can accomplish by ourselves without assistance from others, the better off we are. We are told to excel in spite of the group, as if dependency in intergroup interaction were a negative thing. Within our culture, there is a tendency to attribute our success (i.e., accomplishments) entirely to ourselves individually (i.e., through "hard work and perseverance"); however, we are also quick to blame our failures on the larger group as a way to avoid personal responsibility. When we evaluate concepts relative to an individual's success or failure, we typically evaluate the positive characteristic in reference to the person and the failures of the individual to the group, company or community to which the individual identifies with. Put more simply, we tend to take individual credit for our accomplishments and attribute blame to the group for our failures.

Furthermore, within the individualistic culture, we often fail to evaluate an individual's success with respect to their relationship and position in groups or a large community. This is critical because so often (as many successful persons will tell you), an individual can only become successful through the support and encouragement that he or she gets from family (as emphasized in the collectivistic cultures), work, or a group of friends. Attributions to the self and "individual accomplishments" are

88

typical responses from the individualistic culture and contradict those characteristics and values of the collectivistic culture. Furthermore, the criteria that we use in measuring how "successful" an individual has become is typically done relative to their income and types of possessions—not necessarily to group affiliation. Note all of these terms and characteristics refer to success, typically by oneself, at the exclusion of the group or the community.

This chapter will emphasize the importance in how different cultures emphasize group (collectivistic) ideology versus individualistic behaviors and attitudes in relation to group performance. We will also explore how the concept of "community involvement" and volunteer behaviors has declined as a result of the strong emphasis on individualistic behaviors. Furthermore, we will discuss several examples of how collectivistic cultures can actually reduce ethnocentric tendencies and increase ethnic assimilation by encouraging all groups of individuals to work and play together and emphasize communication in the process.

The History of Collectivism and Individualistic Theory in the United States

Historically, the United States has created a culture of fierce independence as a means of establishing autonomy and freedom. The constitution of the United States and the Declaration of Independence emphasize basic individual freedom as the underlying foundation to the creation of human rights. Thus, our history as Americans has been created with a strong emphasis on our right to exercise independence (i.e., "Live Free or Die"), and this strong will for independence has resulted in a strong belief that doing things by ourselves, without the need for assistance (or control) of others is an ideal cultural value and belief system. The individualistic culture continued throughout the late eighteenth and early nineteenth century in the United States when individuals migrated out to the West to develop farming and agricultural skills. Living free and independent of government control was the dream of many pioneers in America, and the vast stretches of land parcels that were literally given away by the government further exacerbated the drive for autonomy and independence. It is clear then, through our history and development as a nation that individualism has been the foundation of the development of the Western culture and emphasizes individual freedoms reflected within our relationships with others.

Despite the numerous advantages of teaching individuals to think, behave and interact within a highly individualistic manner, there are several limitations to individualistic cultures that may influence how we relate to others within a variety of social and professional situations. For example, people who have incorporated a collectivistic philosophy and who are more group oriented are more likely to view their behaviors as part of the context within the group itself and consider the ramifications of their behaviors within the community (Miller, 1994). Furthermore, research has consistently demonstrated that when individuals have been exposed to collectivistic cultures, they are less likely to engage in hostile acts due to competitive behaviors and exhibit cooperative and collaborative styles of interaction (Phinney, 1996).

Individualistic cultures, such as those in the United States, Western Europe and even Canada, have emphasized the norm of internality, where not only are individuals considered to be responsible for their behaviors, but that they can control most events occurring in various facets of their lives. For example, in these countries, individuals are assumed to control events relative to their health (such as obesity) and substance abuse (such as alcoholism) and are more likely to be held personally responsible for controlling these disorders. Conversely, individuals from the collectivistic cultures emphasize group membership and how the group itself has shaped individual behaviors (Triandis, 1990; Morris & Pang, 1994). Groups in collectivistic cultures take greater responsibility in helping the individual to recover from a variety of problems and share in their belief that individuals can recover from their problems and use these experiences to help others within the group.

The individualistic culture often appears very desirable to many people because it offers them things for their individual advantage and often this occurs at the expense of the group. The problem with the advantages that are often associated with individualistic success is that it comes with a cost — the cost usually being the effort of the group that the individual belongs to and identifies with.

The collectivistic culture encourages individuals to not think as individuals but rather to focus on the welfare of the group itself. Furthermore, collectivistic cultures emphasize the significant and potential strengths of the group when people combine their skills together to solve specific problems. Individuals working from the collectivistic culture are also more likely to focus their identity with particular groups that they belong to, whereas the persons from the individualistic culture first place priority in emphasizing themselves, the things that they own (such as expensive cars) as a means of establishing their identity through a process that is referred to as "conspicuous consumption." Thus, collectivistic individuals identify with their own particular (i.e., ethnic or religious) group and emphasize their efforts to the group itself. The individual's identity becomes the identity of the group. Conversely, the individual from a highly individualistic culture obtains their own identity typically at the expense or cost of the group and achieves goals outside of group assistance. The identity of the individual is determined by the identity of the group. Conversely, the identity of the individuals from individualistic cultures is inherently separate from the group. Additionally, often identity and meaning from the individualistic culture is determined by ownership of things, not through partnerships with others.

Persons who have been acculturated to individualistic cultures are highly competitive with each other and view others as blocking their ability to achieve goals rather than using them as resources to help them achieve success. Even conflict resolution has been influenced by the differences between the individualistic and collectivistic cultures, where persons who have been reared in individualistic cultures are more likely to insult other individuals, whereas the individuals from the collectivistic cultures insult the group or family itself (Semin & Rubini, 1990). Children who are exposed to models who egregiously display individualistic styles of behaviors are also significantly more likely to incorporate egoistic (self-centered) styles of interaction as opposed to playing with others and using other individuals as resources to achieve a mutually desirable goal.

Media today strongly encourage youths to "go it alone" and "get what one can out of life," but the problem is that with this type of philosophy individuals are succeeding in life at the cost of others, not as a result of cooperative behaviors. Individuals who resort to a form of "any means necessary" to excel in their careers or schoolwork typically create a highly competitive environment where trust and cooperation are essentially nonexistent. In professional sports, for example, superstar athletes characterize team sports such as basketball and baseball. These superstar athletes typically, unfortunately, do not display the advantages of using teammates to win games; rather they focus on techniques to enhance and improve their performance, their image, and their incomes, typically at the cost of other players.

When Professional Sports and the Collectivistic Culture Collide

An excellent example of how the individualistic and collectivistic cultures may clash in today's society addresses the problem of team sports with individual superstar players. Professional baseball and basketball are very popular sports (*team* sports) today and have become strongly influenced by the individualistic culture. Some individuals have even compared sports superstars as being an American equivalent to the British royalty. Unfortunately, many highly successful superstar athletes also disregard the concepts that are critical to successful team sports. Individuals who are more group-oriented and collectivistic seek out team-oriented sports, such as volleyball or football and those who are individualistic seek out sports that require little interaction or dependency on others, such as swimming or golf (Larry, Wheeler & Jenkins, 1986).

Some of the superstar athletes have become so focused on winning that they seem to forget that they are participating in a team sport such as baseball or football. Many highly successful athletes refuse to train with their teammates and even practice without having team trainers or coaches present — hardly the description of a true team sport.

Why do superstar athletes play on a team when they essentially are individual athletes? In many ways these superstar athletes have unfortunately become trapped into playing team sports. They play tremendously well as an individual and have exceptional skills as an individual athlete, but are actually limited in their style of play by their teammates. One famous NBA basketball player in 2007 even earned over 80 points in one game but still his team lost the game because of an inability to embrace the collectivistic philosophy into his game — teamwork! The excesses of an individualistic culture such as ours have permeated sports and in some cases have created a schism that seems impossible to reconnect.

Furthermore, the problems with egoistic styles of behaviors that occur in professional team sports distorts the values and the advantages of how others may play because it prevents them from valuable interaction and practice with other players. The advantages of the collectivistic philosophy as demonstrated by the concept of team sports is just that — individuals joining together as a team to play as one group. Collectively and exponentially the skills, aptitudes and talents of ten individuals become combined into a far greater strength than ten. Groups and teams take on a singular identity and talent that far exceeds what a disjointed group of ten individuals could accomplish. It is no wonder that despite the greatness of some of the individual superstar athletes in athletic competition within the individualistic culture, their teams still lose games.

Rather than demanding 60, 70 or more points per game, superstar athletes should focus on working collectively with others, helping them to refine their skills so the overall team could be most successful. Additionally, rather than one individual working for the benefit of the team, all team members need to be working collectively for a common goal. A term that refers to the dynamic force of all team members working together is *collective self-efficacy.*

Unfortunately, examples of the negative effects of egregious individualistic styles of play in sports are all too common. It is not uncommon today to hear superstar athletes complaining about their teammates during media interviews or denigrate the teams coaching style. However, relative to our discussion of the benefits and costs of individualistic versus collectivistic behaviors, egoistic superstar styles of play can be devastating in any team sport and especially detrimental on the morale of the other players. What happens to our youth who witness such exorbitant and egoistic styles of play under the pretext of "good team sports"? What messages do we send young athletes when egoistic styles of play dominate the world of sports with media, attention and money? The message being sent to young athletes is that doing everything on your own, even at the expense of team members, is the key to success.

The message we should be sending out is how much stronger, resilient and talented *all* of the players could be if true teamwork were to occur during both practice and competitive games. Teams in the truest sense of the word should be designed to allow all players to work as a unit and capitalize their inherent strengths by using the skills of each player. When this process does not occur in sports (or in other types of groups), teams will not be playing up to their true potential and lose games.

Parenting Styles and Changing Individualistic Orientation to Collectivistic Orientation: Does a Critical Period Exist?

Our discussion thus far in this chapter has been in addressing the consequences of egoistic behaviors that are frequently demonstrated within the individualistic culture. We should also point out that attitudes and behaviors addressing group work or individualism are essentially learned phenomena — teachers, parents and educators can effectively point out the numerous advantages when we work together as a team or single unit. An important question to address within the collectivistic culture and individualistic culture is in how to teach the value and benefits of collectivism and when is it most appropriate to do so? Does a "critical period" emerge when children are most susceptible to learning the value of sharing and giving in a collectivistic group?

Creating Individualistic Attitudes in Children via Self-Entitlement Parenting Styles

Our discussion of individualistic and collectivistic styles of behaviors has addressed how our relationships with other people can influence our own personal and professional lives. When people live within a highly individualistic culture, their emphasis is more about their own advancement and how groups (such as the community) can benefit them directly. Similarly, we have addressed the negative ramifications of this particular culture and style of living as being particularly taxing on the community and society because individuals rely exclusively and depend on the group for their own personal gain and advantage rather than contributing to the group. Conversely, the advantages of the collectivistic culture are numerous as the society and community can actually gain and develop when individuals devote their time and volunteer their efforts to improving the larger group.

Our discussion of different types of collectivistic behaviors (i.e., community service work, gardening at a community college, volunteerism, and altruistic behaviors) has emphasized the critical role of the importance of the larger group and community and how important it is for individuals to look beyond their own short-term benefits and to focus on working with others cooperatively for the overall long term benefit of the group. No group, community or society can function adequately if a particular proportion of the members are living within the individualistic culture; we are already witnessing the economic negative ramifications of the egoistic and individualistic culture by businesses and social services collapsing because too many people "expect" things to be done for them. This self-expectation that one "deserves" to have certain privileges provided by society and that we are "entitled" to services provided by the community becomes the epitome of the individualistic culture and has been entitled to be a self-serving and self-entitlement culture. But where does this self-entitlement culture develop and how can we prevent it from manifesting further in our society?

How then are collectivistic or individualistic attitudes learned? In many cases in our culture today, parents are teaching children to avoid responsibility for themselves by teaching them to expect others to do what they themselves should be doing. The relationship between the evolution of the individualistic attitude begins with an expectation of what others should be providing for them. This can occur in academics and education, personal health, or in personal relationships with others.

Teaching Children Dependency and Self-Entitlement Attitudes: How to Get What You Want without Even Trying

An important topic of this chapter is in exploring how the individualistic or collectivistic cultures and attitudes have emerged — are there different kinds of things that we can do to enhance and facilitate the development of the collectivistic philosophy among younger people? Important questions now emerge regarding the relationship between these two very diverse forms of cultural attitudes:

- How can cultures influence the attitudes and behaviors of individuals to shape their expectancies of what they should be *contributing* to a community as opposed to what they may *expect* from a community, regardless of one's role within the community?
- What is the best type or form of relationship or ratio between the collectivistic and individualistic society? Similar to the relationship between altruists and opportunists in any society, is there an ideal relationship between givers (collectivists) and takers (individualists) in our culture?
- Can teachers and parents teach and encourage children to adopt some of the behaviors and attitudes that are positively correlated with the collectivistic culture?
- What are the variables that shape and influence behaviors and attitudes among people — both children and adults that ultimately contribute to collectivistic and individualistic behaviors?
- Is behavior a genetically controlled factor, predetermined at birth

through genetics where our behaviors simply "unfold" depending on various environmental circumstances?

In order to first truly understand how collectivistic and individualistic ideologies take shape, we first must briefly review how attitudes are learned and how they influence personality. A current leading theory that describes the process of learning and behavior addresses the role of biology and genetics. To a large degree, what we do as well as our how our attitudes are developed is primarily a result of what we biologically inherit from our parents through genotype. If this theory holds true, then how our attitudes become shaped and influenced would be a result primarily of genetic inheritance and deoxyribonucleic acid (DNA)—but this perhaps may be an oversimplification. Increasing research shows that we may "inherit" predispositions that lead to kindness and empathy (Davis, Luce, & Kraus, 1994) and in some cases arguments have been made for genetic inheritance of an "altruistic gene" (Rushton, Russell, & Wells, 1984). This information is critical in our understanding of the development of the collectivistic culture and philosophy, because if it is indeed possible to *inherit* genetic predispositions towards helpful and cooperative behaviors, we can clearly make an argument that supports the hypothesis that collectivistic cultures exist because they are inheritable traits and have served an adaptive purpose for the larger good of society (a topic that Robert Trivers [1971] refers to as "reciprocal altruism" ["you help me now and at some later point, I will help you"]).

A second leading theory that describes how our behaviors and attitudes become shaped and developed is not so much through inheritance, but rather through our experiences and what we learn through rewards and punishments. This theory certainly is not new, and has been discussed literally for centuries, dating back to Aristotle, John Locke and Jean Jacques Rousseau. John Locke, famous for his analogy of the human personality as a "tabula rosa," described learning as emerging from four basic paradigms: learning by association, learning by systems of rewards and punishments, learning by imitation, and learning by simple repetition. John Locke's views, dating back to the sixteenth century, disputed the current philosophy that infants came equipped in the world with vast knowledge (i.e., "preformationism").

The Development of Collectivism through Association

The laws of association simply argue that people learn to associate one form of a behavior with another, and after repeated pairings, one stimulus elicits a second stimulus. The concepts of collectivism may be learned through the processes of association, where children associate positive characteristics with the group (i.e., security, strength, acceptance and encouragement) with their own individual behaviors. In this sense, the fundamental characteristics that are associated with collectivism become associated with positive behaviors so that group concepts now become associated with success and encouragement. When children have become frequently exposed to the many positive experiences that are commonly associated with group behaviors, such as teamwork and cooperative group work in academic settings, they soon learn to capitalize and make use of the numerous advantages that are associated with the collectivistic philosophy. Additionally, they begin to view the group as a variety of resources and eventually their personal identity merges with the group itself and is not separate from the group.

The Development of Collectivism through Rewards and Punishments: Children Repeat Behaviors That Produce Positive Consequences

A basic law in psychology addresses the frequency of behaviors as a result of the consequences of our actions. Positive consequences to a specific behavior often result in that behavior being repeated. An example of a situation that may yield higher frequencies of collectivistic behaviors may include parents who reward their children for engaging in various group activities, such as community service group work or volunteerism. When parents play a more active role in their children's behaviors and are able to reward children for participating in group activities and community activities, their children will not only become more socially conscious and aware of the needs of others, they will also develop a more collectivistic attitude in their responsibilities to society. Thus, the parent's relationship with the child can play a critical role in the formation of collectivistic attitudes and group functions in the community.

The Development of Collectivism through Imitation: Children Repeating What They See

One of the most basic and fundamental laws in psychology is that children are most likely to repeat those behaviors that they see, especially if the behaviors are demonstrated by what they consider to be a positive role model (i.e., parents, older siblings, sports stars or movie heroes). It is very common today to hear parents describe to their children the value and importance of sharing and engaging in positive and cooperative styles of play. These recommendations certainly sound nice and are words of wisdom that we all can live by. However, a common problem with parents in their relationships with their children is that they are not engaging in the behaviors that they are describing.

Very often parents may provide children with mixed messages where children witness highly competitive and individualistic behaviors while parents provide contradictory suggestions. Comments such as "share your toys" and "play for the fun of the game, don't worry about winning" sound nice, but when children see (and hear) their parents jeering sports officials or referees, they are very much aware of and sensitive to these hypocritical comments. The best way to promote the collectivistic ideology to children (and adolescents) in everyday behaviors is to simply set yourself as a positive role model, one who actually "walks the walk" and engages in the positive behaviors that you recommend to your children.

The advantages of teaching children collectivistic styles of interaction with other children (such as siblings or other children in school or daycare) cannot be underestimated. When children see positive role models and figures in their lives engage in collectivistic behaviors (i.e., such as helping and prosocial behaviors for the group), then they will be significantly more likely to participate in groups and respond favorably by contributing to the group itself. When communities and societies lack collectivistic inhabitants, then the community is less likely to be responsive to the individual needs of the members of the community. Children who are exposed to the advantages of the collectivistic philosophy are significantly more likely to participate in group activities that are designed to help others, thereby improving how individuals within the community relate and interact with one another. When individuals who comprise the group are happier and stronger, then the community itself becomes stronger and more resilient. Thus, helping others within the collectivistic society ultimately helps the individual, and the relationships between the individual and the group become prosocially reciprocal. This belief system is reflected in the old adage: "Help others and you help yourself."

Conversely, when highly individualistic members dominate a community, there is less prosocial and community work that is designed to help others because the emphasis is towards the self and not the group. Because of a lack of a sense of community responsibility and willingness to work with others, the group that is comprised by individualists becomes inherently weaker and less likely to engage in activities that are socially designed or group oriented.

What are some of the more specific things that parents can do to encourage collectivistic behaviors among children? Parents can reward children for showing more cooperative teamwork when playing sports. For example, if your child is playing baseball and one child is experiencing problems in catching or hitting the ball, you (as the role model) can help out by volunteering or making suggestions to the child. When children actually see the behaviors that contribute to the collectivistic ideology or philosophy being demonstrated by a role model (such as a parent or older sibling), they perceive this as very desirable and the right thing to do and will be more like a team player in the future.

The Development of Collectivism through Repetition: Learning Positive Habits

Sometimes learning may not occur from the more traditional methods that we have been discussing. Sometimes children do not learn from watching positive role models, by association or through systems of rewards and punishments. With younger children, John Locke notes that learning may be most effective when it is done in a very routine and organized manner. In some cases (especially with the more mundane and routine tasks, such as daily chores) John Locke noted that learning becomes most effective with routine structure and repetitive schedules—doing things over and over again until the child has incorporated the activity almost as a reflex or daily activity. For example, teaching children that their routine for the day is in getting up on time, washing up and getting dressed, brushing their teeth, and going to school is a complicated task that takes a period of time for children to mold into. Repetition and consistent performance relative to structure and activities is a very important component to learning, according to Locke, as children eventually begin to intuitively "know what they need to be doing" during various times of the day. A child, for example, who regularly comes home from school at 3:30 pm should know from his past schedule and routine behaviors that he first needs to do his homework and then he can engage in his leisurely activities. Without structure and routine activities, children will lack the ability to delay gratification, which is a critical function during early childhood.

A third (and more plausible) description would be the interactionist perspective, where both elements of the genetic and environmentalist perspectives merge together to describe unique forms of behaviors—both collectivistic and individualistic. The interactionist perspective argues that both elements of genetics as well as environmental characteristics shape the personality and behavior of the child. Some parents actually engage in dialogue with their children and explain why things need to be done. This style of parenting is described as the "authoritative" style of parenting and is considered to be one of the most effective types of parenting because research has shown when children are provided with explanations why things need to be done, they are more likely to comply (Baumrind, 1991a).

This chapter has focused on the advantages of the collectivistic philosophy and how collectivism influences group performance, children's behaviors with others and parenting styles. More importantly, however, is the fact that we have identified key methods in teaching children the value of group work that is typically seen in community service work. The collectivistic philosophy and ideology is a critical determinant that influences everyday behaviors and our attitudes that shape individual and group behaviors. We have also described the important relationship between collectivistic philosophies and cultures and ethnocentrism, where those cultures that rank highest in collectivistic traits also show the lowest ethnocentric beliefs in diverse cultures. It is no accident that those cultures dominated by the collectivistic ideology also rank the lowest in ethnocentric attitudes. Collectivistic cultures and belief systems by their very nature are highly inclusive and group-oriented and do not rank or categorize individuals by ethnicity, color, or economic status.

The collectivistic society is one that embraces diversity to its own advantage, where all individuals make a unique fit and contribution to the well-being, structure and development of the community. When individuals view their identity as part of the group, the context and style of what they do change dramatically. Individuals within the collectivistic group feel that the group itself becomes their own personal and professional identity and want to contribute to the group in their own way. The ability to contribute to the group relative to collectivism results in a stronger sense of self and self-esteem. The stronger the collectivistic philosophy is among the group inhabitants, then the greater the potential each person has in achieving their individual goals. Thus, the relationship between collectivism, personal self-esteem and productivity is reciprocal, where the more one feels a part of the group or community, the better one feels about oneself and the more one will contribute or give back to the group. Collectivistic behaviors are designed to benefit all people who comprise the group itself, and these changes lead individuals to engage in more prosocial and cooperative behaviors.

8

Reducing Prejudice and Discrimination via Interdependency

One of the most important topics that currently face our society today is how discrimination influences intergroup relationships and how the behaviors of people in ethnically diverse communities communicate and relate to one another. Conflicts involving the lack of effective integration within multiethnic society are increasing ("Latino Group Rips T.V.'s Hate Speech," *The Daily News*, February 1, 2008) without programs offering new techniques in reducing ethnic violence. Indeed, the central theme and thesis of this text is in addressing the positive influences of group work and community service work in reducing ethnic conflict among diverse groups of individuals. Unfortunately, conflict is a very real and a very serious issue among various minority ethnic groups. In many communities, members of different ethnic groups frequently engage in hate crimes against each other. *The Los Angeles Times* (January 31, 2008) reported that hate crimes have increased among Hispanic and African American individuals, often resulting in random shootings ("Cross-racial shootings spark fear in Monrovia"). It is critical, now more than ever, to identify community-related activities that can help reduce ethnic conflict and improve communication among ethnically diverse communities.

A second recurring theme of this text is in identifying several mechanisms that are available to use within our communities and societies as a means of reducing ethnic conflict. One point that we have already hopefully established thus far is that while the negative aspects of discrimination and prejudice are learned phenomena through our interactions with various individuals, we are in fact capable of "unlearning" negative or counterproductive behaviors and replacing them with more adaptive and productive behaviors and attitudes. Human behaviors are capable of changing if individuals are motivated enough and if they have incentives to change.

One of the most effective weapons that we have today in combating the negative ramifications of ethnocentrism and discrimination is something that all people innately possess— the desire to engage in helpful and cooperative behaviors within the community. This is not something that needs to be learned or developed, but rather something that we all possess and can be manifested when small proactive groups work together for a common cause that benefits all persons. When individuals of different class or ethnicity put their efforts together in working towards a common and mutually identified goal, their relationships become enhanced with each other and an important ingredient begins to emerge that is critical to group assimilation — the development of *interdependency*.

Group interdependency is a concept that allows individual group members to see how each person may become a vital link and asset to the group itself. Group interdependency is the social lubricant that facilitates interethnic communication and progress towards social, professional and economic goals. Furthermore, a contributing factor to ethnic hostility is a misperception of what other groups represent and that ethnically different groups are somehow inherently different from each other. When we realize that ethnically diverse groups of individuals often share many of the same goals that we do— such as better schools for our children, better health care and welfare systems, and healthy living conditions, we tend to work more cooperatively so we may all achieve these mutually desirable goals.

When we realize and see the important contributions that each group member is capable of making to the group, our attitudes and relationships among each other improve significantly. One key mechanism that facilitates the development of interdependency through group work is community service work. The foundation of community service work is achieved through the development of interdependency — providing methods and opportunities within the community to allow all persons to work together and contribute in some way to improve the many segments of society. The famous ego psychologist Alfred Adler (1929) argued that all persons begin their lives as infants in a very psychologically inferior state and the only way we can achieve a sense of competency and self-esteem within the ego state is through the discovery of something we may excel in. Once these skills and attributes become developed, we are capable of providing something of value to be used by others, and this opportunity of providing goods through our skills gives us a sense of self-worth that facilitates our relationships with various people of the community.

Are Discriminatory Behaviors and Prejudice Inevitable among Ethnically Diverse Groups?

Are discrimination, prejudice and ethnic hostility inevitable among diverse groups? If you believe that humans possess free will and choice and are rational creatures, then the answer is clearly "no." Fundamentalists and reductionistic thinking would argue that certain aspects of behavior are immutable and transfixed. Freud, for example, would clearly fall into this category by maintaining the tragic thesis of "Man's inhumanity to Man"—how aggression and human conflict are as inevitable as the sun rising each morning. Just as Darwin noted, "Biology is our destiny," so too did Freud agree that human behavior is destined to conflict, war and strife ("Anatomy is destiny" or "The aim of all life is ... Death.").

These theorists argued that behaviors are essentially instinctual and that humans have no choice but to drive each other to the point of extinction. Freud in his theory of *thanatos* discusses the "death instinct" as an inevitable drive towards our own destruction and Darwin describes genetic variation and adaptation as key elements to our survival, and how aggression was a very desirable (and necessary) trait that helped humans ward off predators. While it may be true that some individuals are in fact biologically or genetically predisposed to be more aggressive in their interactions with others, we are still capable of analyzing and modifying our behaviors based on self-analysis and introspection. Humans control their behaviors and are capable of rational thinking that ultimately defines their future.

However formidable these theories are, humans still have rational free will and choice in their behaviors. Humans may have become "genetically predisposed" to behave in certain ways given certain environmental conditions, but ultimately the rational choice is ours in actually carrying out the good or bad behaviors. If you believe this fundamental distinction between the Freudians and the Darwinians, then you can also believe that discrimination and prejudice are learned behaviors that may be modified under desirable environmental learning conditions. An important component of this chapter is introducing some key psychological theories that will facilitate group development. One such theory is the achievement of interdependency through collaborative group work and community service work. When people feel "linked" together and work cooperatively, then we are more inclined to increase our activities with each other and increase communication among in-group and out-group members.

Discrimination is learned through several sources, and the prejudice refers to learned attitudes towards groups. If something (positive or negative) is capable of being learned, then it can be "unlearned." How ethnically diverse groups interact as well as the quality of the relationships that different groups have with each other is dependent to a large degree in how much contact the groups have with each other. We know that when groups view each other in similar terms and share common experiences, then the rate of ethnocentric ideology and discrimination decreases significantly (Tajfel, 1981; 1982). We will now explore some of the theories explaining the development of discrimination and prejudice and how community service work can reduce these problems. There are six current theories that explain the functions of prejudice and how it influences our relationships with others in society:

- Ego Vulnerability: When groups threaten our feelings of self-worth;
- Shortages of Natural Resources: "We all need to eat";
- Ethnic Classifications: "They're different from us";
- Ultimate Attribution Error (Pettigrew, 1979);
- Social Identity Theory (Tajfel & Turner, 1986); and
- Stereotype Threat

Ego Vulnerability: When Others' Success Is Perceived as a Threat to the Self

Most individuals will probably tell you that they are very happy (at least superficially) when someone (friend or stranger) succeeds at some important activity, such as earning a well-deserved promotion or graduating from school. Furthermore, research also suggests that individuals of one group (i.e., classified as the "dominant" or in-group) typically want to see *their* group perceived as successful and portrayed in a successful and ideal perspective (Tajfel & Turner, 1986). However, when different groups (i.e., non-dominant groups), such as an ethnic minority group, are perceived as somehow becoming a threat to how the dominant group, our attitudes and behaviors then change dramatically. Animosity and even hostility begin to emerge between the groups as one group becomes threatened by the emergence of the other group. This threat may not necessarily be perceived in terms of personal safety, but in more general terms the overall economic factors that are associated with success and education.

When different groups ("out-groups") groups begin to dominate the pre-existing group, then balance becomes affected, and this newly created imbalance often results hostility. The new minority group that is becoming more dominant in society now becomes the scapegoat of hostility because of the perception that resources and employment are being "taken away." The result is tragically characterized by increased conflict and violence. This hostility among dominant groups and non-dominant groups is the foundation of prejudice because people typically begin to categorize members of the other group as all being alike.

An additional factor that has been linked to prejudice and discrimination is that of status and positive "in-group" identification. When members of the dominant group perceive the minority group as threatening in terms of status or income, resentment towards the minority group grows significantly. This increase in resentment to groups based on ethnicity or in some cases gender (Faludi, 1992) has been shown to be the basis of most cases of discrimination where individuals of the dominant group felt their status, hierarchy or income being challenged. It further follows that as minority groups increase in their advancement to jobs, schools and income, greater opposition from the dominant group grows towards programs and social policies that have been designed for equality (i.e., affirmative action programs).

Numerous research studies have documented the universal tendency of people to criticize groups who are perceived to pose some form of a threat to self-esteem. This discrimination may include ethnic discrimination as well as gender discrimination. In an interesting study conducted by Rudman and Fairchild (2004), researchers were able to increase levels of gender discrimination among women who were portrayed as being talented computer or video game players. The male subjects expressed more hostility towards the groups of women who were depicted as being good players in a traditionally male-dominant activity (computer games). Thus, the prejudice developed among the male video players because of a new group (women) who were violating the previously dominated male boundaries of computer games.

Shortages of Natural Resources: Realistic Conflict Theory

Humans, by nature, design and evolution, are highly competitive creatures. Many individuals will claim they are simply not competitive by nature (i.e., "it doesn't matter to me who wins or loses") but ultimately when individual survival is at stake, all humans will compete to survive. A very contemporary theory addressing prejudice today is referred to as the realistic conflict theory or natural resources theory as a fundamental factor that is a contributing factor to prejudice and discrimination. To a large degree, the quality and context of our relationships with others is determined by the availability of necessary resources for our own survival. When these resources (such as food, water, housing and so forth) are in plentiful supply, our relationships are generally positive and friendly. However, as increasing demands on these resources develop, the hostilities among groups increase as we perceive the non-dominant group taking something that belongs to us.

As our precious and limited resources are becoming increasingly limited due to population explosions and poor agricultural and urban planning, there is an increasing strain on natural resources. This strain is manifested through our relationships with individuals who happen to share our resources. For example, fresh water from the Colorado River is being drained by both Americans and our Mexican neighbors to the south. As agricultural needs increase for fresh water, hostility and conflicts have developed over the border addressing water rights. Currently in California a very contentious topic is in creating a border that is designed to keep undocumented immigrants out of California. Ethnic hostility, resentment and even hate crimes have been positively correlated with shortages of natural resources and economic resources (Hovland & Sears, 1940). As the natural resources that we rely on become increasingly scarce, we are beginning to see increases in crimes relative to specific ethnic groups. Unfortunately, a common reaction to shortages of these critical resources by the dominant group is to seek out minority groups as the scapegoat or responsible party primarily for consuming or using resources that are in short supply.

As living space (i.e., affordable housing), resources and jobs are becoming increasingly limited in California, there has also been a significant increase in hate crimes against those groups of individuals (i.e., recent immigrants) who are perceived as primarily responsible in taking them away. Numerous studies have documented the tragic correlation between a declining economy and increasing number of hate crimes against the non-dominant (Hovland & Sears, 1940). In their classic research, these authors discovered a disturbing trend (inverse correlation) among a declining economy and significant increase in lynching. As the price of cotton decreased, the numbers of lynching among African Americans significantly increased; as the price of cotton increased, the lynching decreased.

Ethnic Re-categorization: "It's Us versus Them"

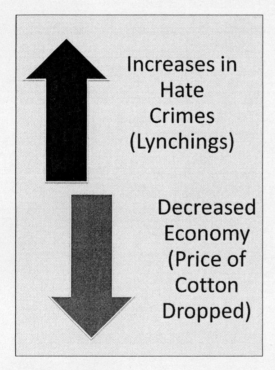

Increases in Hate Crimes (Lynchings)

Decreased Economy (Price of Cotton Dropped)

It is actually more difficult to *not* like someone than it is to like them. In order to not like someone, we often have to offer some form of justification, no matter how fabricated or ridiculous the reason may become. People also often need to keep reminding themselves why they do not like someone or some group, and this needs to be continually refreshed as time goes by. Essentially we need to create reasons to foster the animosity and dislike. It also requires a good memory to remember (over time) why you think you dislike someone. You may also remember your parents or teachers telling you as a child it takes more muscles in your face to frown than it does to smile. In the case of discrimination and prejudice, individuals need to have some reason or justification of their rejection for others that may be based entirely on ethnicity, gender, religion or sexual orientation.

It isn't enough today to simply say, "I don't like him or her because they happen to be of ethnicity X or Y," or that they may be practicing the wrong religion. Perhaps, many years ago, in a less politically correct era, someone may have made reference to their prejudice in this manner. Perhaps the most primitive and most basic mechanism and function of discrimination and prejudice simply comes from the fact that people separate others into basic groups—the "good" (dominant) group and the "bad" (minority or non-dominant) group. When we are able to justify our discrimination by placing ethnically diverse individuals into convenient differing classification systems (such as "us" versus "them"), we are simply trying to rationalize a very basic and primitive human function of human interaction. When we feel as though we have more in common with a particular group and we perceive that they are more like us in different ways (i.e., political or religious views, SES, etc.) we are significantly more likely to perceive them as one of us and respond favorably to them. Indeed, the basis of most forms of discrimination and ethnic hostility is typically due to a misperception of differences that we have with other groups of individuals. In a sense, then, we create a division or dichotomy between those who are more like us (i.e., the "we" group) as opposed to those who we perceive as somehow being different from us (i.e., the "they" group).

Overcoming the We-They Dichotomy: Discovering We Are They

When groups of individuals are separated by the "us versus them" philosophy, prejudice continues to develop because they are maintaining a very real psychological as well as physical distance between groups. The dominant group typically enjoys greater resources and controls how the resources are spent. The dominant group also typically lives in a more affluent area that is also geographically separate from the non-dominant minority group. The physical distance as economic difference creates a separatist climate that feeds the discrimination between the two groups. When ethnically different groups of individuals lack contact with each other and believe that they are inherently different (i.e., "privileged") from the minority group, a strong tendency to separate begins to emerge. There also is an increasing urge or drive to expose the non-dominant group as being inferior in several ways which also further exacerbates the distinction of "us versus them."

This psychological and physical separation thus becomes the foundation of discriminatory actions and violence and pulls groups characterized by race away from each other. The key to overcoming the "us versus them" culture that feeds ethnic violence is simply in renouncing the distinctions and salient differences that are based on ethnicity and to help focus more on common links and similarities with each other. Furthermore, groups realize that despite their phenotypical differences, they have more in common with each other and in many ways are very much alike.

Thus, the basis of discrimination from the "us versus them" philosophy continues to dominate our society because the minority group is *de facto* separated from the dominant group, thereby preventing effective interaction between the two groups. The groups remain separate from each other in many facets of daily interaction, such as professional, business, social and recreational activities. When groups become separated by class or ethnicity they become very easy to classify into in-groups or out-groups and the classification process itself becomes the catalyst for separatist and discriminatory behaviors. The minority group becomes differentiated into the "they" component by becoming secularized and differentiated in everything from living arrangements to the foods that are eaten to health care, education, and so on. Thus, a significant component and causal factor associated with prejudice and discrimination is economic in nature, and this economic and class distinction builds the wall that separates "us" from "them."

Perhaps the most effective way to counteract the "us versus them" philosophy is by "tearing down the economic wall" that creates the division of classes. Only through increased contact and communication among all group members, where the dominant group usually discovers that they have significantly more in common with the minority group that they previously anticipated, can prejudice become significantly reduced. When this occurs, "they" become "we." Not surprisingly, individuals who are considered to be part of the dominant group are viewed more favorably than members of the non-dominant group (Lambert, 1995).

The psychological phenomenon of strong preferences for individuals who are considered to be part of the dominant ("us") group has profound implications as the basis and foundation of prejudice and discrimination. For example, a very common social psychological phenomenon where we tend to make very flattering attributions towards ourselves (and others considered to be in the "us" group) and conversely negative attributions towards those in the non-dominant group ("them") is referred to as the ultimate attribution error (Pettigew, 1979).

The psychological dynamics are very similar when comparing the ultimate attribution error with the foundations of prejudice and discrimination. In many cases of discrimination and prejudice, distinctions are drawn because of the misperception that one group (in-group — the group that we identify with) is inherently better that the other group that we do not identify with (out-group). In both situations, we perceive *ourselves* (i.e., ultimate attribution error) or our *group* (i.e., dominant or in-group) differently and somehow better than groups that we do not identify with, and this by definition is the foundation of discrimination and prejudice. Think, for example, the last time you watched a baseball game where you clearly had a favorite team, and your friend favored the opposing team. Usually your observations towards your team tended to be favorable (the "us" team) and the success from the team is attributed to skill; conversely, success from the opposing team ("them") is generally attributed to luck.

Social Identity Theory

Our fifth theory addressing the problem of discrimination and prejudice is perhaps the most recent and universal theory. The social identity theory was originally proposed by Tajfel and Turner (1986) and describes the universal tendency for individuals to categorize themselves positively and often at the expense of other groups. Tajfel further argues that a continuing reason why prejudice and discrimination are pervasive problems in communities is because of the increases in self-esteem that some individuals achieve by deriding non-dominant groups. When we criticize minority group members we implicitly develop a stronger attachment and identification to the group that we perceive as ours or the dominant group.

In other words, we all have a basic and primary need to view not only ourselves positively and our perceived group favorably, we also tend to do this at the expense and cost of the other non-dominant (minority) group. This should sound relatively familiar to the "us versus them" (social categorization) theory, but there is one significant difference with the social identity theory. In the social identity theory, individuals often realize that it is wrong to criticize other groups simply as a way to enhance how we feel about ourselves. Thus, in the social categorization theory we continually balance out our own primary egoistic need to enhance our feelings of self-worth while (often simultaneously) criticizing other individuals in the non-dominant group.

This very basic and primitive need to view our own accomplishments and self-worth more positively at the cost of the non-dominant group has very important ramifications as a fundamental cause of prejudice and discrimination (Spears, Doosje, & Ellemers, 1999). While most people certainly try to be justice-oriented and fair when considering skills and talents with other individuals, even despite this effort towards a "color-blind" approach, our own biases towards individual favoritism at the cost of non-dominant group members still exist. For example, who deserves to get that competitive promotion at work if both candidates are relatively equal in all other aspects besides ethnicity? What should be the criteria in accepting students of color in a highly competitive college or university? What about the criteria in granting amnesty to undocumented workers?

Stereotype Threat: The Dominant Group and Perceived Negative Influences of Performance

The interesting response to each of these very divisive questions falls on one central theme — security in your own cultural identity. Numerous research studies conducted by social psychologists suggests that when we (as members of the dominant group) feel most secure with who we are as members within our group we are significantly less likely to engage in ethnic hostility or discrimination (see, for example, Hornsey & Hogg, 2000). Significant research has supported the hypothesis that when members of the dominant group feel most secure about their own cultural, ethnic and economic identity they are more likely to view diversity in a positive and supportive manner. One suggestion in reducing ethnic conflict among different groups of people within the community is perhaps in helping them to first feel secure about their own ethnic identity and then work together by focusing on what each group has in common with other groups within the community. Identify what the common problems are for each group and then form a "multicultural think tank" in developing strategies and problem-solving solutions. This way not only improves our ability to work together more cooperatively but also improves relationships among the many different ethnic groups within the community.

However, if you feel threatened by your own ethnic or cultural identity (the "non-dominant" group is now dominant) you may respond negatively towards other persons from different groups applying for "your" promotion and many college students may have ambivalent feelings towards principles involving affirmative action when they realize that their acceptance to that prestigious college now may be taken by a member of the non-dominant group. However, when we recognize what we have in common with members of all groups (dominant and non-dominant), we are significantly more likely to view these persons from all groups more positively. Thus, a central theme of our text has been to identify the methods that help us to discover our strengths and similarities with each other and to work cooperatively and collaboratively with each other. Without utilizing this critical philosophy in our society, we are destined to ethnic conflict and division.

We have identified six of the most common factors that are associated with ethnic conflict, prejudice and discrimination:

1. Ego vulnerability;
2. Shortages of natural resources;
3. Ethnic classification systems;
4. Ultimate attribution error;
5. Social identity theory; and
6. Stereotype threat.

The good news is that we are not destined to continuously engage in conflict and repeat our past mistakes—humans *can* change if they put their minds to it.

This chapter will now conclude with five positive theories that all have one goal in common: how to first identify, then reduce and ultimately eliminate prejudice. These five theories are also based on common principles—things that we can all do and effectively put into action if we only put our minds to it.

Going APE over Community Service Work:

a. **Activate** change in your community through community service work: work together for a common goal;
b. **Participate** in community events and working together via increased contact;
c. **Educate** yourself: reclassify the boundaries—we're more similar than different. Understand different perspectives;
   • *Cognitive Changes*: Just say yes to working together;
   • *Social Learning Theory*: It all starts with you!

Activate: What Community
Service Work Is

The thesis and primary purpose of this text has been in addressing techniques in improving interethnic relationships, reducing ethnocentrism and conflict via community service work and interdependency. Interdependency has been a central theme throughout this text as the key factor necessary in bringing ethnically diverse groups together. Interdependency has been the glue keeping groups of individuals together since our early evolutionary history and remains a vital component to the development of positive relationships with individuals. One of the most effective activities that can establish interdependency is community service work. When individuals work cooperatively via community service work, they are afforded ample opportunities to meet with and communicate with a broad range of diverse individuals that helps us to recognize our similarities with each other.

Community service work has been the central theme in this text that describes the value and importance in having community group members work cooperatively to solve persistent problems within the community. Innercity problems, such as crime, poverty and poor educational institutions, are central to the scope of community service work. These difficult issues affect all members of the community, and they can only be resolved by a concerted effort from members of the community. This means not asking, "Who is going to do this?" but rather "How can we work together to find a solution?"

What Community
Service Work Is Not

Community service work is not just a transitional fad or a group of individuals getting together occasionally and picking up trash at a park or handing out food to the homeless. Community service work is not a photo op for an opportunistic celebrity, politician or model who hands out food baskets during the holiday season when the cameras are ready. Community service work *should* address the central problems within a community and tap into the resources that all people inherently possess. Community service work should also capitalize on the numerous skills that all people have and discover the numerous hidden talents and potential that bring people together. Community service is a very positive and even contagious activity where people enjoy working together for the sole purpose of helping others and their community. Research shows that community service work is not effective by just having people occasionally get together merely out of obligation, but rather only becomes effective when people coordinate their skills towards a common goal.

Individuals engaging in community service work typically do so out of some form of social obligation, often feeling that it is the right thing to do. They may not actually be aware of the dynamic and positively reinforcing interpersonal (and intrapersonal) changes that commonly occur with community service work. When people of different ethnic groups realize that they depend on others and others depend on them, their attitudes become significantly more constructive and positive and interethnic relationships also improve significantly (Aronson, 1986; Brewer & Gaertner, 2001). Many individuals who have engaged in previous community service work continue their participation primarily because of these dynamic and positive changes that are typically associated with their volunteer efforts.

What Community Service Can Be

Community service work represents the many positive things that all societies and groups can develop and changes the individualistic concept of the self into the collectivistic concept of the group — regardless of color or ethnic identification. The benefits of community service work are numerous and not only can have positive consequences in solving problems relative to the community (i.e., reducing graffiti, teaching skills to the homeless, etc.) but perhaps more importantly can have positive effects in how people relate to each other. In our research addressing community service work and reductions in ethnocentrism (Hoffman, in press), my colleagues and I were able to establish the value and importance of ethnically diverse groups of individuals working cooperatively in improving the physical appearance of a community college for minority students. After six months of collaborative work where volunteers within the community, students at the college, as well as students from higher levels of education (Pepperdine University and California State University Northridge) all worked on a campus garden, student relationships changed significantly. Not only did the level of communication with students of various ethnic and economic classes improve as the study progressed, but perhaps more importantly we saw significant changes in the reductions of ethnocentrism. A pre-and post-test design was conducted where the participants were first measured on levels of ethnocentrism prior to any community service work. Mentors were assigned to the experimental group condition and post-test scores of ethnocentrism were significantly reduced: (2.95), t (10) = -12.70, (p < .0001).

The results of this study and community service work in general are very encouraging in our effort to improve the quality of working relationships within ethnically diverse communities. We have discussed several theories that describe how interethnic hostility and divisiveness develops, but more importantly we had identified several theories that can mollify and even eliminate ethnocentrism if people are willing to work cooperatively together. Perhaps the most serious problem plaguing our community today is prejudice and discrimination, with ethnocentrism as the foundation of ethnic violence. An important component of community service work is in allowing all members of the community an opportunity to work cooperatively with each other and to use all skills and talents that people possess.

A related topic that is similar to the community service philosophy is commonly referred to as the jigsaw approach (Johnson & Johnson, 2003; Slavin, 1989). The jigsaw approach utilizes the skills that individuals have not only within the community, but students learning cooperatively in the classroom (Hoffman, 1995) where cooperation (not competition) is the key element that contributes to interdependency. The jigsaw approach typically gives students a limited amount of time to develop a key strategy to solving a problem given to the entire classroom by the instructor. Students are randomly selected to (interethnic) groups and, in order to achieve a good grade, they must all work cooperatively together. Just being placed in ethnically mixed groups is not enough to reduce ethnic hostility — students (and community members in general) must be faced with a common problem and work together to achieve a solution. When these variables develop and merge together, the results are usually very positive.

We have also learned that these traits and characteristics are learned phenomena and that they may be readily "unlearned" if the community activity and service work allows members to work cooperatively with each other. Most importantly, however, is the fact that we need to rediscover our "need to be needed" through the social fabric of interdependency. The realization of the mutual need of interdependency allows us to discover the similarities that we all share with one another.

Participate: Working Together
via Increased Contact

Increased contact (sometimes referred to as the contact hypothesis or "intimate contact" [Brislin, 1993]) argues that much exposure or contact with diverse groups helps all individuals to improve communication and reduce negative stereotypes that are often associated with minority groups. Similar to the principles in the community service activities, the contact hypothesis argues that exposure and working cooperatively towards mutual goals often tends to reduce friction and hostility that often occurs with groups that lack contact with each other.

The key point to emphasize in the contact hypothesis is that all groups, however diverse or different in cultural backgrounds, need to be working toward a common goal that benefits everyone involved in the effort. Examples of ideal goals that have been highly successful in the contact hypothesis have been:

• Improvements in housing — building more affordable housing districts for low income families;
• Creating community service gardens where all members of the community grow a variety of different vegetables to be distributed to the homeless shelters. During World War II, many American families created the now famous "victory gardens" because the majority of vegetables and fruits went overseas to the soldiers;
• Improvements in the physical structures of schools in low-income areas. Families from different cultural backgrounds and economic class may consider donating one weekend a month to improve schools, parks, and recreational facilities which often become targets of blight and graffiti.

Increased contact with two groups who have a history of conflict can improve relations simply by the realization of similarities that the two groups inevitably share. Contact used in this context can not only mean working together, such as a mutual task or community project, but in the simplest cases verbalization and communication with other members of different groups. Research shows that in many cases, just confiding and talking about our fears and emotions can elicit positive feelings towards different groups (Brislin, 1993). The frequency of increased contact will also result in the transition from separate categories ("them" versus "us") to a more homogeneous identity ("We are all community members").

Think for a moment the last time you may have had a negative encounter with someone — it may have been a disagreement or argument over a topic that both of you feel strongly about — and how you felt about that situation and that particular person after the incident. Chances are probably very good that you rehearsed the incident over and over again trying to identify the sources and reasons of the disagreement. You may have felt that the individual you were arguing with perhaps did not fully understand or appreciate your position on a particular topic. In time, you may have relaxed and wished to communicate more effectively with this person who misunderstood your position. With increased contact hypothesis, the more often we come in contact with others, the more able we are to clarify who we are and reach compromises with individuals who we formerly perceived as our enemies.

More importantly, however, is the fact that with increased contact with different groups we are better able to understand behaviors that may have historically been problematic in relationships and we are also better able to communicate our positions to different groups. Increased contact hypothesis affords individuals more opportunities to identify common links with each group and to establish new bonds of friendships with diverse groups.

Conversely, the lack of frequent contact with different groups sets the stage and foundation for animosity and resentment toward the groups. These hypothetical situations are very similar to how animosity towards other minority groups may develop — because of the lack of contact that we may have with other groups based on ethnicity, economics or religion, we tend to foster more negative (usually incorrect) stereotypes that are associated with that particular group. The best way to help alleviate and eliminate these often incorrect stereotypes is simple contact — working on joint or mutual projects together or organizing colloquia in ethnically diverse student groups in high schools or colleges that help to identify and correct the stereotypes are both excellent examples of how increased contact and communication may improve our relationships among diverse groups within the community.

Perhaps one of the most contentious topics of in-group versus out-group identification involves radical religious groups. Terrorist groups proclaiming religious affiliation and carrying out the "works of God" by literally destroying and bombing societies and killing innocent victims today are increasingly threatening our society. Quite ironically, religion is quickly becoming one of the most commonly cited reasons why individuals engage in terrorist acts and murder. Historically the Protestants and the Catholics of Northern Ireland have had a very tragic and destructive relationship with one another, each group becoming intolerant of the existence of the other group. Increases in dialogue through painstaking negotiations and working towards successful communication to find common ground (very difficult with orthodox religions) can still be successful and has significantly improved the relationship between these two groups (Paolini e al., 2004).

Educate Yourself: Reclassifying the Boundaries — We're More Similar Than Different — Understanding Different Perspectives — Challenge Stereotypes!

Educating yourself means more than reading books—it means learning and understanding more about people and putting yourself in their perspective. Understanding diversity means taking a closer look at each group and trying to recognize and respect the differences that do exist relative to ethnicity and experiences. Sometimes the best way to communicate is through listening to the unique and challenging experiences that many individuals may have relative to their personal history. Reclassifying the boundaries of ethnicity and ethnic identification means simply to drop the need to classify individuals in terms of race or ethnicity to move more towards grouping individuals in similar terms and context.

Ethnicity and Stereotype Threat

When is the last time you really evaluated whether or not you treat people differently based on outward appearances? If you are like most people, we tend to think that how we treat others is usually in a fair and non-biased manner, but research does suggest that all of us (minority or non-minority groups) do tend to engage in stereotypical thinking from time to time. We bring up stereotypes in this chapter because stereotypes essentially become the foundation of discrimination and bias. Virtually everyone has stereotypes because they have been shown to be vital cognitive processing mechanisms and help us to process information on a daily basis. Many times, however, groups do respond to our negative biases and this only confirms the stereotype even further. A term that is used more commonly in describing this event is referred to as stereotype threat.

Stereotype threat refers to a form of a self-fulfilling prophecy, where usually minority group members may respond or perform poorly on an academic or cognitive skills test not because of inferior ability, but rather because they are responding to the perceived dominant group's expectation of performance. For example, researchers Steele and Aronson (1995) discovered that when African American students are requested to place ethnic identity on an examination paper with their name, scores significantly decrease. The same phenomenon is not true among Caucasian Americans taking similar tests. Why is this? Why do only some groups (typically minority groups) underperform when they are aware that their race or ethnicity is being identified or called into question? According to Steele and Aronson, the answer lies in the expectation of how individuals are to behave or perform. This is why it is critical for educators to have realistic yet challenging expectations for the students that they are teaching. As we are all very much aware, teacher expectations have a profound influence on student performance (Rosenthal & Jacobson, 1968).

Unfortunately, the stereotype threat is not limited to race and ethnicity. Gender has also become a frequent topic of stereotype threat. For example, in cultures that still have strong double standards relative to acceptable male and female behaviors, women often underperform on mathematical tests when they are reminded of their gender (Shih, Pittinsky, Ambady, 1999). However, when Asian American women are reminded of the culture (i.e., Asians typically outperform other groups in sciences and math), their skills significantly increase. The stereotype threat is a key concept to consider when engaged with members of different ethnic groups, because we may see differences in cognitive or intellectual performance that may be due to differences in testing situations rather than individual or group differences in cognition or intelligence.

The foundation of discrimination rests on the assumption that members of different ethnic groups are inherently different from the dominant group in other aspects. When we reclassify and reorganize how we view different groups and when we consider our similarities with people, we reduce the need to stereotype groups based on these perceived differences. When we are able to view all persons as equal to one another, we are eliminating separatist classification systems and creating what Dovidio and colleagues (1998) refer to as a "common in-group model." When we reclassify individuals who were previously from the out-group, we now identify with them because we are focusing on similar characteristics that the groups have with one another and this tends to produce more positive feelings in general. The out-group literally becomes our group.

The basis and inherent foundation of all stereotypes, then, is primarily due to incorrect or false suppositions of some groups (usually out-group members) over other groups (usually dominant group members). These suppositions transform themselves and influence behaviors typically via ethnic polarization (different groups, based on ethnicity, separate from each other). After the initial separation, bias and hostility grow from one group toward the other group, and the third outcome usually is either over discrimination and ultimately ethnic conflict:

Cognitive Changes: Just Say Yes to Working Together

During the 1980s in the Reagan administration there was a tremendous emphasis in reducing substance abuse and drug abuse in many different communities. The plan was very simple yet highly effective and appealed to many different people because of the simplicity that it proposed to all members of society. The campaign slogan was "Just Say No to Drugs" and it was highly successful. Sometime later this highly effective slogan was used for reducing sexually transmitted diseases ("Just Say No to Unsafe Sex") and was also successful in changing behaviors and the culture associated with unsafe practices.

THE EVOLUTION OF DISCRIMINATION

"Psychological Separation" = *Perceptions* of Differences Among Groups

↓

Groups Become Physically Separated or Polarized

↓

Bias / Hostility Projected to Out-Group Members Typically via the Media and Literature

↓

Economic Discrimination: Jobs Become Unavailable for Out-Group Members

↓

Ethnic Conflict (tension among groups): Out-Group Members Accused of "Taking Our Jobs"

↓

Ethnic Hate Crimes

Similar to these successful slogans of the 1980s era, these cognitive changes may be applicable in reducing prejudice and discrimination. "Just Say No to Racism" may initially sound trite and superficial, but if enough people within the community begin to support (and practice) what these cognitive rehearsal cues emphasize, it is very possible to see significant reductions in discriminatory behaviors. Many negative stereotypes based on minority figures exist simply due to our own tendency to process information in the easiest manner, what many researchers refer to as the "cognitive miser" effect. If we practice equality and fairness in our daily interactions with members of different groups, we can avoid relying on the negative stereotypes that has been the foundation of prejudice and discrimination. People (especially younger persons, such as children) can be taught that relying on negative stereotypes and generalizing are key elements to the formation and development of prejudice. More importantly, however, is the fact that parents and educators can teach children very simple key behaviors to avoid using negative stereotypes in the first place. Successful methods in utilizing this strategy may be in emphasizing each person to focus on the strengths and positive characteristics that all persons of all groups possess and to cognitively rehearse these positive attributes during future interaction with each minority group.

The key question to ask is whether negative stereotypes that are associated with race and ethnicity can change through cognitive rehearsal, and the answer clearly is yes in many examples of research. Kawakami and colleagues (2000) demonstrated that when subjects were instructed to associate either positive or negative stereotypes with different ethnic groups, their reliance and speed with assigning positive or negative stereotypes with different ethnic groups changed significantly. This research is especially important relative to stereotypes and the processing of cognitive information because it shows that negative stereotypes pertaining to ethnic minority groups may in fact be modified and in some cases even eliminated. When negative stereotypes are replaced with positive information, the styles of communication improve and the use of negative stereotypes decreases. These results confirm what previous research has suggested, that when we cognitively rehearse and train ourselves not to associate negative stereotypes with members of minority groups we can do so effectively.

Social Learning Theory:
Teaching Children Diversity

Research has consistently demonstrated that the vast majority of anti-social or aggressive behaviors are learned through a variety of daily sources, such as the media, entertainment industry and role models (Bandura, Ross, & Ross, 1963). But what does the social learning theory have to do with prejudice, discrimination, and ethnic interaction in our society today? According to recent research addressing the influences of what children are exposed to via the media and the formation of attitudes, the social learning theory actually has a profound influence on not only what is learned among individuals, but our attitudes as well as the context of our relationships with others in our community.

Many researchers have demonstrated that the foundation of discrimination develops through the formation of negative stereotypes that are often learned simply by exposure to media that perpetuates these stereotypes as well as role models emphasizing these stereotypes through film and media (Towles-Schwen & Fazio, 2001). Additionally, researchers have demonstrated a very strong correlation between levels of parental prejudice with children having similar negative views of minority groups—what children *see* and *hear* from their parents (as well as other perceived role models) does in fact influence what children do in future types of situations (Turner, 1991; Wright et al., 1997).

Simply stated, if we want our children and young people within our community to engage in behaviors that are non-biased and egalitarian with members of different ethnic groups, then we need to do the same thing in our daily interactions with different groups of people. Children do in fact process even the most subtle forms of negativism displayed towards minority groups, and may perceive inappropriate humor directed towards minority groups as being truthful and accurate.

The key question to address is in how can we teach children and people in general to not rely on the negative stereotypes that they may have learned through their interactions with others? One effective method is in simply educating those individuals holding strong levels of prejudice and bias and showing how destructive and inaccurate their views are in relation to how ethnically diverse groups interact and communicate with each other. In many situations individuals who may harbor negative stereotypes relative to ethnic minority groups may simply just need to realize that their discriminatory practices are in fact harmful to others. If this self-realization is in fact possible, then the regret and remorse that is typically experienced (often referred to as "collective guilt") will serve as a catalyst in engaging further discrimination and help them in avoiding similar types of prejudice in the future (Branscombe, Doosje, & McGarty, 2002).

Finally, we should also emphasize the individual benefits of a community that practices egalitarian principles, ethnic fairness and cooperation and avoids negative stereotypes to the different groups that comprise the community. Subjective reports of overall happiness and contentment that one has had over his or her personal and professional life are significantly higher among those individuals who avoid embracing the negative stereotypes that are commonly associated with ethnic minority groups (Feagin & McKinney, 2003). In other words, treating people fairly, without incorporating negative ethnic stereotypes or prejudice is not only the right thing to do within the community, but will also help you to feel better individually about yourself.

We began this chapter emphasizing the importance of interdependency as the key ingredient in reducing ethnic discrimination and prejudice. Interdependency allows ethnically diverse individuals to emphasize what their common links are and how positive cooperation remains the most powerful and successful element in group dynamics. Taken together, these findings provide powerful evidence that interethnic communities that practice effective communication skills with each other and avoid the often damaging and destructive negative stereotypes that are commonly associated with ethnically diverse groups are more productive, interactive with each other, and in general show more positive characteristics than ethnically polarized communities.

9

Keeping It Real

THE INFLUENCE OF TECHNOLOGY
ON THE QUALITY OF INTERPERSONAL
AND GROUP RELATIONSHIPS

Technology (like so many other things in our lives) has the potential to be used highly effectively in our efforts to educate people and to improve our overall quality of living, or it can become counterproductive to education and detrimental in the quality of our relationships with others. It can certainly facilitate communication among different groups, as well as improve our levels of academic performance. It can be a very valuable asset in teaching basic skills and helping people to better understand each other. Unfortunately, if it is not used wisely, it can also have highly negative consequences and result in groups becoming alienated from one another and even contribute to aggression among groups.

How often have you become familiar with a product that was very useful for a short period of time and you felt that you could no longer function without it. Cell phones, digital cameras, emails and text messaging sent across the world and modern technology in general seem to be rapidly replacing old-fashioned direct contact and communication with our family and friends. Do not, however, become beguiled by the temporary charm and charisma that these new gadgets often produce. Do not assume that technology and machines can replace the spontaneous intelligence and altruistic support that is often characterized by human interaction. The virtue of authentic human interaction manifests itself *especially* in times of crisis and turmoil — but it does exist (and has always existed) within the community itself. The problem that we address in this chapter is that the sense of community and interpersonal interaction that has evolved with people for literally thousands of years is now becoming threatened by a false sense of autonomy that is perpetuated by technology. More opportunities of community engagement are giving way to independent activities that unfortunately devolve into separation and alienation from the group itself.

What is happening within our society is that technology is preventing humans from engaging in prosocial behaviors and from interacting with each other on a deep and personal level. Technology has even been associated with increases in conflict among groups of individuals and deters effective human interaction (Henline, 2006). Communities are often plagued by crime and poverty, preventing people from engaging in meaningful interaction with each other and a greater reliance on technology from what people once did for one another. This isolation from each other and living in fear creates a sense of autonomy and detachment that is the antithesis of interdependency within the community. One needs only to wait until the next natural disaster or crisis to see how quickly people scramble for actual human contact when machines fail them. Occasionally we need to be reminded that ultimately we only have each other and we need to rediscover the importance of authentic human interaction.

A major premise of this text is that ethnically diverse groups of individuals in society are becoming increasingly polarized for a variety of reasons, and because of this increased polarity, interethnic tensions and conflict are more likely to develop within a variety of environments where these groups meet. Furthermore, while limited polarization among different ethnic groups is common among multiethnic communities, an important component of this text is in exploring what techniques exist that may facilitate interethnic assimilation and how to best implement these strategies through community service work and group work within different societies.

In some cases, modern technology is promoting an autonomous belief system where individuals may believe that they can exist in total harmony by themselves and exclude others. For example, why bother in getting to know your neighbor who lives next door or introducing yourself to other students in a new class when all you need to do is create an online chat line. When you get tired of your new computer pal, all you need to do is simply turn off the computer — simple, easy, and no problems such as emotional involvement. Worse yet, in some cases technology is being used to create websites and chat rooms that encourage and facilitate prejudice and even hate crimes. Technology is only instrumental and effective in helping us function in ethnically diverse communities when we focus on the strengths that each group possesses. Unfortunately, technology can become negatively manipulated to encourage divisiveness and hatred instead of cooperation among diverse groups. In this chapter we will take a closer look at how modern technology can help groups function and work cooperatively together towards goals or encourage ethnic violence.

In other cases, societies are becoming racially separated into groups that have also become separate by economic class and available technology. Compare academic resources (i.e., computers in the classroom) among two very different schools by economic class and you will see better teaching facilities and academic resources in affluent schools and outdated or inferior equipment in the less affluent school systems.

In this text we submit that an inability or refusal to attend to these growing problems will only lead to a further misunderstanding of diversity that can lead to hostility and aggression. As communities are progressively becoming more diverse there should be programs and educational systems that facilitate an understanding of the various cultural characteristics and mores that are associated with distinct ethnic groups. Without these educational techniques that teach members of the community about cultural diversity and the lifestyles that are typically associated with them, problems are certainly likely to follow.

Clearly, most individuals would agree that societies and our world are simultaneously becoming more ethnically diverse and yet (paradoxically) they also are becoming more polarized from each other. The result is numerous smaller groups (enclaves) that are characterized by ethnicity and avoid integration with the dominant group. Modern technology further aids the polarization effect, as the enclaves and other groups in society use technology to communicate with others rather than direct or person-to-person interaction. For example, now individuals need only to call on their cell phones or text message someone that they already know rather than introduce themselves to new people in a new situation (i.e., classroom situations or social events). Video games and electronic recreational systems that simulate group or team sports further exacerbate these problems among children by portraying simulations of team or group activities that are essentially individual activities. Children only think that they are playing and interacting with other children in their virtual world whereas in reality they become more dependent on the technology and lose sight of the value of authentic human interaction.

Technology Replacing
Human Interaction

More and more often, individuals are resorting to electronic technology as a means of replacing traditional forms of human interaction and communication. Thus, students in an ethnically diverse class or community event may feel compelled to call their friends on cell phones or text messages rather than introduce themselves to individuals of a culturally diverse background. Technology, therefore, is becomingly increasingly responsible for what we call "ethnic insulation" as opposed to proactive interaction with members of different ethnic groups. Additionally, increases in diversity do not necessarily guarantee increases in assimilation and integration of those diverse groups. Therefore, it is critical in communities that serve diverse groups to better understand the tools that may improve communication and a better understanding of each other.

In this chapter we will emphasize both the positive and negative potential that technology can influence within group relations and education. We will first discuss the potentially negative ramifications of technology in-group and interpersonal relations and then we will focus on the positive components. What does technology have to do with how ethnically diverse groups communicate and relate among one another? Actually, technology influences our relationships with others as well as our communication with people on a daily basis. A disturbing trend that is developing more frequently not only in higher education, but in a variety of different social situations, is the increasing tendency for technology not to help but actually to *interfere* with human communication, group relationships and group interaction.

The Miscommunication
of Cell Phones

Cell phones for example, were designed to enhance and facilitate communication, and (when used correctly) they still serve this purpose. Now many individuals use cell phones in lieu of actual (i.e., *in vivo*) conversations with other people. Ask many individuals if they actually prefer using cell phones over personal interaction and communication, and the vast majority will tell you that they prefer cell phones over personal communication (CSUN student survey, 2008). It is not uncommon for many family members to admit that they have used cell phones to contact family members who were even in the same house. Text messaging and computerized chat rooms now are becoming the norm (not the exception) for individuals to meet and socialize and engage in virtual relationships. Now individuals do not even have to leave the sanctity of their own home to do something as basic as grocery shopping — with the click of the mouse a stranger delivers the food right to the door.

Are these the reasons why technology has been developed? Probably not, as now technology is contributing to how groups of individuals have become alienated from one another, children and adolescents prefer video games to physical recreation, and the computer and various websites have replaced our need for actual one-on-one interaction. In this chapter we will identify what things we can do to reverse this disturbing trend and revise technology back to the point where it can actually help groups to interact and interrelate with one another.

Modern technology traditionally has been designed for the purpose of making our lives easier and more functional and has been structured to provide us (supposedly) with more leisure time. More generally, the purpose of technology is to facilitate and improve our overall standards and quality of living. Unfortunately, much of our technology today is currently being misused to the point that it is rapidly becoming counterproductive not only in our individual lives but in how groups function and relate to one another. Think for a moment, when the last time was that you received an unsolicited message (commonly referred to as "spam") or was prevented from working due to constant "pop up" advertisements? In a recent survey, over 72 percent of those interviewed indicated the worst habit among cell phone use was being exposed to "loud conversations." Today it is even common for schoolchildren to carry conversations with their friends via cell phones and cell phones have become as standard as the traditional lunchbox. In the same survey, nearly 70 percent of the respondents indicated that they have seen poor cell phone habits *daily* (emphasis mine; www.microsoft.com/smallbusiness).

Our reason for including technology in this text is to consider how the excessive use of cell phones, text messaging, and emails can depersonalize our relationships.

The Cell Phone Effect:
Reach Out and Disturb Someone

Think back for a moment the last time that you were either watching a movie in public or eating at a restaurant with friends. You may have even been waiting for a flight at an airport and reading a newspaper. Chances are very good that with all three of these activities, someone very close to you was using a cell phone to the point that his or her use became very distracting (perhaps even annoying) to you. They are laughing and talking so loud on their cell phones that they were probably oblivious to their annoying effects on everyone else within fifty feet. You could no longer concentrate on what you were reading or doing because someone was engaged in a loud conversation with another person — you are drawn into the conversation because you have no choice. You cannot prevent yourself from listening (it's like telling someone not to look with their eyes open) and you were becoming very annoyed at the lack of courtesy being displayed by the cell phone user. Why were you annoyed? Most probably you were annoyed because your space, your area, your privacy have all been stolen away from you. Certainly you could leave the area, but in some situations you cannot (i.e., in an airplane waiting to be taxied).

Defenders of inconsiderate cell phone use justify the use of the devices by saying our society has changed so much now that it is common, if not necessary, to use these devices just about everywhere (including the bathroom). They further maintain that they have just as much a right to use these devices as you have to your own privacy. But the real issue that we wish to discuss here is not so much how annoying the technological devices has become, *but rather how they are changing our relationships with people and how we form our relationships and communication styles with others.* Whatever the reasons, current technology is advancing far beyond our means and ability to maintain etiquette. The result is more and more individuals relying on technology to replace actual human interaction that does have significant ramifications in the overall quality of how we feel about ourselves as well as others.

Recent empirical evidence seems to confirm our hypothesis that modern technology is contributing to the deterioration of our relationships and quality of direct communication with others. In a recent study, Hoffman and colleagues (2006) explored the influence of a community service activity (outdoor gardening program) with the perception of the need to use electronic technology, such as a cell phone or text messaging. Ten community college students were randomly selected and administered a questionnaire exploring the need and frequency of use of their cell phones and text messaging devices. Sample questions included: "I don't really think I could function without using my cell phone at least several times during the day" or "I prefer using electronic technology over talking to people directly." A second focus of the study was to evaluate student perceptions regarding the need to participate in a community service or volunteer program that was designed to help individuals in lower socioeconomic environments.

The purpose of the study was to determine if outdoor service learning activities (i.e., a community-based gardening project) would reduce perceptions of the need to use communication devices (i.e., cell phones or text messaging) and increase the likelihood of participating in future volunteer projects. The participants that were used in the study all scored significantly higher on the pre-test, citing both perceptions of need and frequent use of cell phones. Many indicated in the pre-test data that they did not think they "could ever function" without their cell phone and even complained of "cell phone withdrawal" symptoms.

Over the following several months the participants were instructed to participate in the community service gardening program at least two to three hours a week without any influence of electronic technology. During the course of testing, students were instructed to interact and verbalize directly with each other and to "rediscover" the value and benefits of direct communication in an outdoor setting. The results were very encouraging, with a significant decline in self-reports of the need to use cell phones. Additionally, the participants in the study also increased their scores in their opinions of the value of community service learning programs and all indicated that they would participate in future community service or volunteer programs ($p < .001$). Our post-data suggests that the experimental group's mean score of perceived needs for electronic devices (i.e., cell phones, Ipods and headset radios) and technology (14.33) was significantly lower than the control group's mean score (34.00), $t(8) = 5.73$, $p < .05$.

These results are very encouraging because they suggest that once people become sensitized to the misuse of electronic technology, they are quick to make changes to improve their levels of communication with each other and to reassess their values in terms of time and commitment relative to community service volunteer programs. Stated simply, with the onset of technology and information literally at our fingertips, many individuals have become self-involved with their careers and personal relationships and need to explore the bigger picture, the bigger picture of course representing what we may contribute to our community rather than expecting things done for ourselves continually. The subjects in our study indicated that their communication improved with each other significantly and this was only possible to identify when they were removed from the overwhelming environment of technology.

Today even cell phones now come equipped with cameras that also seem to exacerbate the problem of etiquette and appropriate use (see "Camera Phone Etiquette Abuses," CBS News, Tokyo, July 9, 2003). Technology has even allowed workers to give the impression that they are at work when they are not (called the "Shirk Effect"). Email messages may be sent to others around the country to give the appearance that you are working late from your office when in fact you may be home relaxing. Many supervisors are now reporting the misuse of computer technology where computers may answer phones or manipulate email messages to give the impression to the several recipients that "employee Smith" is hard at work at the office late at night when in fact he may be home or having a beer with friends. The bottom line is that when computer technology becomes manipulated to give the impression people are working when they are not, we all lose. When technology is misused, not only the quality of interpersonal relationships becomes negatively affected, but our work ethic also becomes affected in a very detrimental manner.

Cell Phone Use Compromising Education in the Classroom

As an instructor of psychology for over 20 years, I have taught a variety of different psychology courses in different times and styles of teaching. Traditionally longer lectures required the use of one or two different breaks. Ten or fifteen years ago (prior to the introduction of the cell phone *en masse*) it was very common for students to chat during the break. This informal and friendly chat time allowed for students to interact and to familiarize themselves with each other. As most teachers will agree, a class that is more familiar and friendly with each other also affects how the classroom discussions progress. It will also influence how well the course information is covered and how freely students provide personal information relevant to the lecture that always makes for a more interesting and dynamic discussion.

However, since the introduction of the cell phone, students by and large now converse with their friends on cell phones, thereby limiting their interaction with other students in the class. There no longer seems to be a desire for students to mingle with or converse with fellow students enrolled in the same class because, well, to introduce yourself and to get to know different people takes some initiative and some effort. It is simply easier to call someone that you already know and talk when it is convenient for you and to "shut them off" when it is also convenient. Apparently, it has simply become too much work to meet new people today. The academic impact of this growing trend is that students who feel less comfortable with each other in class tend to share less in the classroom discussions and appear somewhat more distant and alienated from one another. Students who remain estranged from one another tend to feel more inhibited in sharing in the discussion sections of the lecture, thereby limiting how the students in the class receive the course material.

The Development of Racist Websites via Technology

Unfortunately there are many individuals who live within the community that use technology to foster hatred towards other groups. In chapter 10 we will discuss the existence of hate groups in more detail, but for now we will briefly mention how technology is used in the development of negative and hate-filled websites. The fact that the internet has facilitated the creation and development of hate groups is indisputable. According to data provided by the Simon Wiesenthal Institute (www.infoplease.com/spot/hatecrimes.html), the number of hate websites ("hate sites") increased from a low of 163 in 1997 to an alarming number of 254 in 1998, and the numbers still continue to grow. What makes hate sites potentially most destructive is the detailed messages that they provide to young persons—such as specific instructions in how to create (and detonate) explosive devices designed for minority groups, how to get to minority groups, and have even provided personal information (i.e., home addresses and phone numbers) that may expedite the destruction to the victim's house.

The Tragedy of the
Oklahoma Bombings

The detailed instructions and procedures of the Oklahoma bombings that were carried out by Timothy McVeigh were provided to him via racist websites. Timothy McVeigh would not have been able to carry out his horrendous activities if he had been prevented from using the internet and hate-filled websites to carry out his crimes. We need stronger laws monitoring the use of websites that carry out hate crimes and more enforcement of the misuse of the internet in general.

Unfortunately, terrorists (both international and domestic) are being provided access with potentially destructive instructions and information that facilitate their ability to carry out their horrific activities. These are clear examples of how technology is rapidly becoming misused to the detriment and destruction of our community and society. Technology via the website unfortunately also facilitates anonymity — it is becoming harder and harder to track down and trace those individuals who are responsible for the development and creation of the hate websites. Currently our laws provide for prosecution of hate crimes only if the crime was conducted on a specific group based on race, religion, ethnicity or sexual identification.

Improving Diversity through
Technology — Multicultural
Videoconference Colloquia

We have been discussing the potentially negative characteristics of the misuse of technology (cell phones, text messaging, and computer use) among individual and group interaction. We will now focus on some of the *positive* uses of technology in helping ethnically diverse groups to interact and assimilate with each other in various situations.

If properly supervised and organized, technology can certainly enhance how groups interrelate and communicate with each other.

Videoconference Colloquia (VCC)

Students who simply read about other groups of individuals, whether they are from the remote Aborigine tribe in Australia or our neighbors residing in our own community, often fail to have an accurate perception of what the different cultures really represent. Several years prior to the technology revolution that wc are now experiencing, students could have read a book or even written a report about different ethnic groups and the culture and way of life. This description would have been educational, but limited in its actual range in providing other students with a realistic picture of what life was really like in that remote culture. With videoconference colloquia students can not only learn about different cultures, they can *experience* it through new technology.

Students ranging from middle school through graduate school who may have limited cultural interaction with ethnically diverse students may organize a videoconference colloquia (hereafter referred to as VCC) in the classroom. The VCC program is an excellent method and very popular approach that is currently being used by many different schools and educational institutions that combines the benefits of technology in helping students in highly remote and culturally geographic regions to introduce themselves to each other and discuss their values, ethics, and cultures with each other. The VCC is one very effective method to eliminate negative stereotypes, biases and myths that may be commonly associated with international (and domestic) ethnic groups.

Imagine for a moment, students living here in the United States sharing educational experiences with students in Iraq, discussing the virtues and benefits of democracy, or students in Nigeria talking with students in the United States about diet and obesity — imagine the rich and vast educational potential that the VCC offers. With the VCC technique, students may engage in a virtual video and cultural seminar with one another and share ideas and values and can actually discover how different groups of people live together. Often students are surprised to discover that the children from Iraq watch many of the same programs on television as children do in the United States. They learn, for example, that their interests and concerns are very similar and this realization helps to reduce the we-they dichotomy that fuels ethnocentric ideology and attitudes.

Cooperative Internet Groups

A second possible idea that effectively incorporates technology with promoting multiculturalism combines the traditional concepts of cooperative (sometimes referred to as collaborative) group work with a modern twist — using the internet. The internet may be used to facilitate collaborative learning styles where students can understand different groups and cultures via internet correspondence. In traditional forms of collaborative group work, clusters or small groups of students work together on a classroom project and share their talents and skills with one another. Often in collaborative group assignments, teachers may award one single grade to the entire group, which tends to serve as an incentive for all students to work cooperatively with each other.

Additionally, cooperative group work is unique in the sense that it typically yields outstanding work because it incorporates the skills and talents of all members into a single focus. When organized correctly, collaborative learning is most effective in learning and serves as an ideal educational tool because all groups of students typically want to share their knowledge with others. Cooperative internet groups can also help individuals who may be experiencing similar problems (i.e., substance abuse) to work together and share their positive experiences via the internet.

Group work traditionally is very effective when individuals who may be suffering from a common problem meet regularly to discuss their issues and share possible resources in addressing the problems. Cooperative internet groups are also very helpful but now members work together on the internet to share not only their problems but ideas and strategies in helping other group members to overcome their problems. The internet now allows students from across the globe to learn and grow together, which ultimately improves interethnic understanding and reduces ethnocentric ideology.

Electronic Individual Correspondence — Technological Penpals

We have been discussing various types of technologies that have had positive influences in diversity and education via *group* work. Groups of individuals work well with each other when goals are clearly established and all people contribute to the solution of the perceived problem. Technology cannot only help groups to function more efficiently but can also help in individual relationships, such as technological penpals. Electronic individual correspondence (sometimes called technological penpals) is the newest form of technology designed to help individuals on a singular or one-on-one basis. Here individuals from around the world can literally meet other people online and share their views and attitudes towards universal problems and establish constructive and positive relationships with one another on an individual basis.

A teacher in high school, for example, may provide an assignment to a class to send an email describing one student's culture, background and interests to another student living in a very geographically remote area. In this manner, students will be able to discuss their family, their culture and their lifestyles with other culturally diverse individuals to better promote understanding. One sample exercise might be for an American student to discuss his or her everyday experiences in school, doing homework, going out with friends as well as their experiences living in a democratic nation. Students living in newly formed democracies (i.e., Iraq) could then share their views with their penpal and exchange attitudes and experiences to promote understanding with people who live in very different cultures.

10

The Paradox of Maintaining Ethnic and Cultural Identity and Assimilating in the Dominant Group

A common dilemma facing many new immigrants (commonly referred to as the out-group members) is in how to assimilate within the dominant culture (in-group) without compromising their ethnic and cultural heritage. Recent studies suggest that one of the biggest hurdles facing new immigrant groups is how to integrate within the community — how they may best fit in while yet maintaining their own sense of ethnic identity and cultural heritage (Hodson & Sorrentino, 2001). For many new immigrant groups who arrive to a new culture, economic survival and adaptation are key factors in the process of successful assimilation. Often members of the non-dominant group want to assimilate and integrate within the dominant culture but lack the knowledge and skills to do so. Many members of the dominant group may actually resent efforts by the non-dominant immigrant group to integrate out of fear — fear of a loss of jobs, housing and economic status. The minority group members are placed in a no-win situation where they become ostracized by the dominant group simply due to ignorance and fear.

The new immigrant group typically needs to maintain cultural ties and practices as a means of maintaining their own heritage, but also need to integrate within the dominant group itself as a means of economic survival. Conversely, members within the dominant group often view the close-knit behaviors of the new immigrant group or enclave as being clannish and even arrogant, and resent the new immigrant group's attitudes as a sign of rejection of dominant group values. A form of psychological distancing develops where out-group and dominant group members begin creating barriers to effective interaction based on misperceptions of each group. Thus begins the problem of assimilation and integration. Proximity and distance increase between the two groups due to misperceptions relative to integration. We maintain, however, that the two concepts of ethnic identity and assimilation within dominant groups are not mutually exclusive concepts. We submit that it is possible for members from different cultures and nationalities to maintain their identity and heritage and to still assimilate within the dominant group culture. Furthermore, in this chapter we hope to address and provide several simple interethnic activities and programs that offer techniques in facilitating group interaction and yet appreciation of ethnic diversity and different cultural heritages.

Cooperation, Community Service Work and the "Gardener's Dilemma"

One effective method in helping minority group members participate and interact with members of the dominant group is community service work. In community service work, all group members contribute towards a common goal. There are actually several different types of community service projects or civic engagement activities that enable diverse groups to work together and share their ideas while promoting unity among ethnically diverse environments. Some individuals work in homeless shelters and provide meals for families and their children. It is considered to be a community service project because members from various ethnic and cultural backgrounds combine their efforts to help prepare temporary living environments and hot meals for the less fortunate.

Creating a beautiful landscape or garden through the combined efforts of people working together is a second example of community service work that helps people to better communicate and understand each other. Enabling and empowering people to discover how their strengths can contribute to society and helping different people to get along better is perhaps an even more important goal of community service work.

What makes community service work highly effective is the fact that all members of the group are contributing towards a mutually important goal. Additionally, perceived out-group members are now perceived to be peers and many common links are developed. In order for community service work to be effective, however, all members within the group must work together (at some individual cost) to achieve their goal. If cooperation is beneficial to all group members, then one may ask why it is not demonstrated more often in in-group settings. The answer lies in the fact that cooperation always requires some amount of individual investment — and with personal and individual investment comes risks. These risks have been categorized in many ways, but the most risk has been described as the prisoner's dilemma. We describe what has been known as the prisoner's dilemma here in this chapter as the gardener's dilemma, where in order for outdoor gardening work to be most successful, all persons must contribute relatively equally in their physical labor in order to maximize the end result: A productive, healthy and well manicured garden.

The Gardener's Dilemma, Cooperation and Community Service Work: Working Together Increases Benefits for Everyone

A major premise of community service work is the inherent condition that groups need to work cooperatively as a means of achieving goals. Without relative reciprocal interaction among the participants, then community service work would be rendered impractical and even counterproductive. Without relatively equal output of work by members within the group, then those who do complete the majority of their work experience resentment and frustration when they perceive others who do not appear to be participating in their fair share of work. This is the antithesis of community service work. Our major premise has been that when all individuals contribute to various group projects in a variety of ways, a sense of interdependency develops where individuals actually feel compelled to work cooperatively and collaboratively with others.

Often many of the participants have commented in their gardening work that their benefit and positive experiences in working in the garden are based (in part) in the observation of all of the group members contributing and working together for a common and shared goal. One recent participant indicated in her journal after working in the garden:

> What was great to see [in the garden area] was that most of the students barely took 20 minutes to finish their lunch.... The mowing students divided up their areas for the rest of the days, the shrubbery students decided to finish another area towards the back of the garden, the students in charge of the vegetables got

right back to work, and I found myself rounding up the girls and starting weeding again. We planted about 30 smaller flowers together and got really excited after looking at the work from a distance. We were so proud and excited after looking at our work from a distance.... I was full of pride and a sense of gratification that the hard work I put in the five hours was there, and I felt elated. I had no idea that I was in for such a meaningful experience through gardening. It goes to show you that when people work hard together for a common goal, it does not matter where you are from or what you do in your everyday life, great work is accomplished.

The prisoner's dilemma is a rather interesting (and common) form of a social dilemma, where each person within a group can maximize their own personal benefit only on the condition that other persons behave in a similar way. In this situation we have utilized a garden area to describe the prisoner's dilemma (or, in this case, gardener's dilemma), where in order for a garden plot to be successfully established, all persons must combine their efforts and work cooperatively together (see figure 10).

For example, if two people (Gardener A and Gardener B) are required to plant a community garden that is one acre in size in a limited period of time, then it is necessary that both individuals maximize their efforts so the goal (planting a one-acre garden) may be accomplished. Conversely, if one person wants to rest and hopes that his or her partner may complete his work, then the garden will not be completed as quickly and, more importantly, animosity builds between the two gardeners. Worse still, if neither of the gardeners engage in any type of work, then nothing is accomplished and no vegetables are planted for the community.

The Gardener's Dilemma

	Gardener B *collaborates*	*Gardener B* *does nothing*
Gardener A *collaborates*	Success! Work is completed efficiently, productivity increases, improved morale and reductions in ethnocentrism result	Gardening work is only half done — some animosity builds among the workeres who complete the project
Gardener A *collaborates*	Gardening work is only half done — some animosity builds among the workeres who complete the project	No work is completed — garden remains unfinished

Community service work rests on the assumption that all people work cooperatively in achieving their goal. As the group nears completion of their goal, the group realizes that their potential and self-efficacy can only be realized when they pool their resources together, a term that is referred to as collective self-efficacy. In the beginning phase of the task, all persons must make commitments that typically involve some form of a sacrifice and require time investment. As the task (in this case, completing the garden) nears completion, the interaction and relationships between members improves, as does the level of collective self-efficacy. As self-efficacy improves, so does the overall perception of increasing one's sense of empowerment not only for himself or herself, but for the community at large.

Collective self-efficacy typically provides a very positive and powerful effect on all group members as tasks near completion because all members discover the inherent value of true cooperative work and its vast potential. As the group-oriented task nears completion, individuals typically improve their relationships with each other due to the frequent and direct contacts that they share with one another. Pettigrew and Tropp (2006) refer to this phenomenon as task-oriented cooperation — a form of cooperative behaviors among groups of individuals who share a mutual responsibility in completing a variety of tasks.

Proximity and Repeated Exposure among Ethnically Diverse Groups: Getting to Know Each Other

Social psychologists have known for years that there are techniques to help different groups of individuals to get along better and actually improve their relationships with each other. Evolutionary psychologists have argued that a clear adaptive mechanism for safety and survival is one where groups show initial reluctance and resistance to newcomers or strangers to the group (Kardong, 2008). Zajonc (2001) supports this concept by noting that humans in general respond negatively to any individual (or new circumstance) as a means of adaptation. However, the more accustomed we become to individuals through repeated exposure, the more likely we are to accept the stranger and feel comfortable with the stranger within our own group.

In many cases, if groups of individuals are simply close to each other in terms of proximity, there is a greater likelihood that the two groups will have more favorable evaluations of each other due to repeated exposure. In some of his classic earlier research, Zajonc (1968) found that repeated exposures to a new or novel stimulus actually resulted in a more favorable or positive evaluation of that stimulus. When addressing group relationships and trying to improve how groups of individuals respond and interact with each other, the first component is in getting the groups *together*. This may be more difficult than it seems—imagine, for example, that you are trying to negotiate or broker a compromise between two people who have been upset with each other for any length of time. Another example may be in trying to get two rival gang members together for a common purpose, such as a community improvement project. It probably would be very difficult (if not dangerous!) to just get the groups together, let alone communicate with each other. Zajonc noted that if two groups displaying conflict or animosity towards each other can somehow simply become exposed to each other, they are more likely to resolve their differences.

The next key element in improving relationships is in creating a situation or environment where each group member feels obligated to attend to some community function or activity, where exposure to each other is most likely to occur. This is the basic premise in community service work, where ethnically diverse groups of individuals meet regularly to achieve a common goal. As the goals become achieved, so does the exposure to each other, thereby serving as what Johnson (2003) refers to as a "social lubricant." Thus, we can see why community service work has become so effective in bringing diverse groups of people together to improve ethnic interaction. Community service work combines the inherent advantages of repeated exposure (members involved in community service work see each other consistently over time), interdependence (group members realize that in order for community service work to be effective, each person must work cooperatively with each other), and finally community service work helps different ethnic groups to assimilate with each other while still maintaining their unique cultural heritage:

Community Service Work

↓

Repeated Exposure and Proximity Increases

↓

Collective Self-Efficacy Increases and Cultural Identity Increases

There are many reasons why community service work and civic engagement have been popular activities over the years. Individuals who work together not only feel better about themselves and their accomplishments, they feel better about those around them and their community members. When people work cooperatively together, they learn more about each other and develop a strong sense of trust — they develop positive feelings about each other through a mechanism that is referred to as repeated exposure.

Techniques in Maintaining Cultural Identity and Assimilation

A primary concern for many new immigrant groups is in maintaining the delicate balance between cultural identity and integration within the dominant group. Many first-generation groups find it especially difficult because they are the newest group to arrive to a new culture. Second and third generations typically assimilate at a much faster pace.

Included are some examples of the most popular assimilation practices that also embrace community service characteristics (figure 10b offers some helpful acculturation "tips" that are easily implemented in educational or community organizations):

• **Community Gardens.** One very popular activity that involves gardening skills and helps to bring people from different ethnic and cultural backgrounds together is in the development of a community garden. Community gardens typically represent each ethnic group's heritage through the display of various plants, shrubs and flowers that are native to the continent of each immigrant group. For example, individuals with African heritage may include tropical plants that are commonly found in West Africa, lotus flowers from Asia, and the eucalyptus variety trees from Australia. In the community service gardening program at Compton College, different students from different geographic regions and even different continents (i.e., Nigeria, Africa, Asia and Australia) have planted trees and flowers that are indigenous to their native countries. One student from Australia planted a eucalyptus tree and several students from Nigeria planted the acacia tree, and students from Asia have planted the Ryukyu tree. Several students from Mexico planted several different varieties of cactus plants and succulent plants which thrive in the arid climate of southern California. The trees and plants provide an ideal mechanism for students from different cultures to share their experiences with each other and to get to know one another, as well as educate each other from different locations of the world.

- **Multicultural Colloquia: An Educational Celebration of Different Cultures and Lifestyles.** Teaching the value and importance in understanding persons from different backgrounds and cultures can actually add to the strength and resiliency of any community. Primary schools, high schools and higher educational institutions in general are excellent environments that may help to educate people about the various cultures of new immigrant groups within the community. Schools may organize poster sessions and create teams of two or more students working together from different cultural backgrounds to help improve their understanding of the culture from each partner within the group. Teachers may intentionally create partnerships among individual students from diverse groups so they may actually learn from each other. The newly formed team may present their findings to the classroom so all students may learn from each other. On a slightly grander scale, if enough faculty are willing to help volunteer their services, instead of a single classroom sponsoring "multicultural colloquia," schools may organize a conference that invites several schools from different areas as a possible theme.
- **Food Fairs.** There is something about food and people that just goes together. Whenever groups of people work together, food always serves as a mechanism to help individuals within the group to relax, communicate and share ideas with each other. Therefore, it should come as no surprise that creating food fairs is an excellent way for members from different ethnic groups to get to know each other by sharing recipes and culinary delights with each other. Encourage members from different backgrounds to cook and prepare foods that are native to each cultural heritage. Create fiestas and community events where members share their backgrounds with each other while preparing meals that are native to each group.
- **Cross-Cultural Penpals.** We have discussed the importance of introducing the benefits of community service work and appreciating different cultures as special topics during childhood and adolescence. Adolescence is a critical period of time where the value of appreciating and respecting topics of cultural diversity should be addressed and discussed in educational environments. Research consistently supports the hypothesis that when children and adolescents are introduced to the importance of cultural diversity via community service work principles, there is a significantly greater likelihood of understanding, appreciation and respect of those principles later in adulthood. One very popular mechanism that allows children and adolescents to learn and

share information from diverse cultures is in the development of electronic penpals. With electronic penpals, students are able to communicate with other students throughout the world in a matter of minutes. The sharing of information relative to one's culture and family history is an excellent way for young persons and adults to correspond and to better understand cultures that are different from our own.

An excellent example for an electronic penpal correspondence program would be for children to correspond with others from areas of the world that have historically become the targets of negative media. In many cases of overt racism and discrimination, minority groups are targeted because of a gross misrepresentation by the media (i.e., terrorism and individuals of Middle Eastern descent). Implementing programs such as the penpal program where young persons are provided with an opportunity to get to know persons from different cultures can be an excellent method to reduce stereotypes that have contributed to animosity and ethnic or religious conflict. Examples of this might include children from Muslim families, children from Iraq, and other countries that have traditionally experienced conflict due to their religious beliefs. In this way, individuals are capable of understanding the "human element" from persons all over the world and avoiding the negative stereotypes that foster racism and hate crimes.

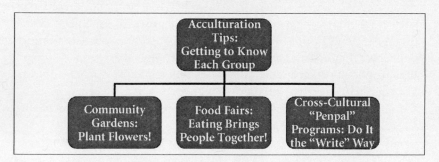

11

Reducing Hate Crimes via Community Service Work in Multiethnic Student Populations

Why Do Hate Crimes Exist?

We began writing this text primarily out of concern for how different ethnic groups show an increasing tendency to become polarized from each other. Not only do we believe that we can significantly reduce levels of overt and covert racism, bigotry and prejudice, but we also believe that we can eliminate hate crimes if we are able to focus on some key psychological principles. Hate crimes exist primarily out of two lethal combinations: fear and ignorance. Ignorance can foster hatred by preventing individuals from effective communication with each other and fear can foster hatred by preventing individuals to accept change in their lives. As long as people believe they can change, then the world can change in a positive way.

Unfortunately, the existence and development of hate crimes in key areas throughout the United States has been progressively increasing within the last decade. In the San Fernando Valley, California, three separate hate crimes were documented in a period of fourteen hours. The locations included Jewish Temples (the Bernard Milken Jewish Community Campus) where a Molotov cocktail was thrown at the Temple (*The Los Angeles Daily News*, February 20, 2008). The same week in California, a young boy living in Oxnard, California, was shot to death because of his sexual orientation. Finally, a Los Angeles Police SWAT Officer (Randall Simmons) was shot and killed February 7, 2008, in Winnetka, California, during a barricaded suspect situation. Unfortunately, these tragic occurrences are more frequent today, with hate crimes and violence as a common theme among ethnically diverse groups. Additionally, violence can also strike out at an individual's religious and sexual orientation. The foundation of discrimination is essentially ignorance based on an individual's ethnicity or sexual or religious orientation. Today, perhaps more than ever before, there is a critical need to address the problems of hate based on a lack of understanding of different groups and how to improve ethnic interaction.

With the increases in ethnic and religious diversity there is a need to educate and promote tolerance among various groups within the community. If we do not promote interethnic skills and appreciation of diversity among students in primary schools and high schools as well as the community, then ethnocentrism and hate crimes will increase.

Throughout our review of research that addresses race relations and ethnic interaction, different ethnic groups have historically maintained positive relationships when each group maintained cohesion with each other and focused on achieving common goals through collaborative efforts with other groups. Schools and communities need to become proactive in their efforts in creating programs that facilitate interethnic activities, such as community service projects, educational activities (i.e., collaborative group work) and recreational activities. The more interaction each group experiences, the less likely conflict may develop among these groups. The quality and the context of our relationships with different groups often depends on environmental and economic conditions that influence how we relate to them — either positively or negatively. For example, groups that engaged in cooperative behaviors and experienced improvements in communication also shared positive experiences in their relationships with each other (Sherif, 1961). Our concern today is that the different types of activities that have historically brought different groups together are becoming increasingly scarce.

Unfortunately, there are fewer opportunities for different groups to share collaborative and civic opportunities with each other that have historically fostered prosocial and positive experiences within the community. Parks, community garden centers and affordable recreational areas traditionally provided to the public are becoming increasingly scarce for a variety of reasons, but the most common is a lack of money available to maintain these areas. Communities and families are finding it increasingly difficult to share time together and this may also contribute to members within the community feeling alienated from one another. We have also cited concerns that increases in ethnocentrism may be correlated with increases in discrimination, anti-immigration sentiment, and even acts of hate crimes that are directed towards various minority groups. Our final and most important topics in this chapter will be in addressing causal factors of hate crimes, the relationship between ethnocentrism and hate crimes and finally how to reduce hate crimes.

If we fail to remain proactive and vigilant in our efforts to reduce ethnocentrism, then ethnically diverse groups are at risk for developing into ethnic aggression and even hate crimes. Hate crimes, discrimination, and prejudice all share one factor in common — they target smaller groups that are perceived as a threat in some way (i.e., economically, intellectually, socially) to the larger or dominant group. Hate crimes, however, go much further than maintaining a separatist or elitist ideology (which is prejudice) or not hiring someone because of his or her ethnicity (which is discrimination). Not hiring someone for employment because of his or her sexual, ethnic or religious orientation is an example of discrimination. Intentionally causing harm to someone else based on and because of these characteristics constitutes the legal definition of a hate crime. Hate crimes are intentional actions designed to physically or psychologically harm other people based on ethnicity, gender, religion or sexual identification. Hate crimes exist because in many ways people learn to hate and are taught to distribute their hate towards specific groups. Hate crimes target typically out group or minority group members and use actual physical aggression or psychological intimidation as tools in carrying out their destructive activity.

We have discussed various theories identifying how prejudice and discrimination develop over time. Infants and children are not born with a tendency to engage in hate crimes, but rather these behaviors develop over time from unhealthy environments or parents that engage in discriminatory behaviors themselves. Often hate crimes are the end result of a disturbing pattern of discrimination and prejudice that starts early in childhood development (see figure 11a):

From the perspective of the individual within the dominant group, soon all out group members take on similar characteristics that begin to make them easier targets as victims of hate crimes, a phenomenon that is referred to in social psychology as out-group homogeneity (i.e., "They all act alike, they all look alike, they're all the same"). This tendency to paint negative stereotypes of members of the out-group with a broad

| Unhealthy Role Models |
| (Parental Discrimination) |
| ↓ |
| Ethnic Polarization |
| ↓ |
| Hate Crimes |

brush often may lead to hate crimes and even ethnic in-group favoritism or ethnocentrism-the tendency to view our own group more positively and preferentially than members of different groups.

Four Psychological Events Must Occur for Hate Crimes to Develop:

(a) *Hate Crimes Are Learned Phenomena.* Perhaps one of the most controversial topics relative to hate crimes, discrimination and prejudice is that of its origin. Where exactly does the hate crime originate? A pessimistic and skeptical view of human nature may believe that the propensity for hatred lies within our own biological destiny. However, some of the more recent literature suggests that hate crimes stem from learned phenomena from the individual's environment. Individuals do not begin their lives hating others; there usually are other factors involved, such as learning and imitating negative stereotypes from others. Children who are exposed to hateful environments targeting persons of color or sexual orientation, for example, learn to retaliate by participating in violent or destructive acts towards these minority groups. Children who are taught to respond with violence towards other groups often are indoctrinated at very young ages and become essentially exposed to principles of hatred toward specific groups. The good news, however, is that if we believe that hate crimes are learned phenomena, then they may be unlearned as well.

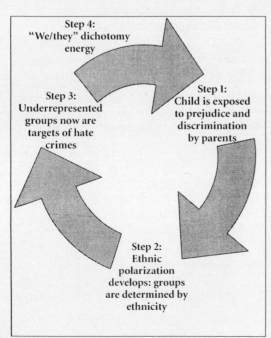

Step 4:
"We/they" dichotomy energy

Step 3:
Underrepresented groups now are targets of hate crimes

Step 1:
Child is exposed to prejudice and discrimination by parents

Step 2:
Ethnic polarization develops: groups are determined by ethnicity

(b) *People who Engage in Hate Crimes Typically Have Low Self-Esteem.*

Individuals often engage in hateful behaviors to feel better about themselves at the expense of an out-group member. They often degrade members of minority groups to seek approval and acceptance from others and require recognition from the dominant group to make themselves feel better. An interesting concept in social psychology is referred to as downward social comparison, where we compare ourselves to those who are less fortunate; we tend to feel better about ourselves. People who have typically do not feel secure in their own self-worth often feel compelled to criticize or demean others at several levels, income, religion, or in this case ethnicity. The key to reducing hate crimes that are caused by low self-esteem is to show the individual how to increase his or her own levels of self-esteem without deriding and criticizing others based on their gender, ethnicity, or economic class.

(c) *The Hate Crime Is Directed towards Any Out-Group or Minority Group Member.* Out-group members may include any minority group based on ethnicity, sexual identification or gender or religious beliefs. Typically when members of the dominant group engage in hate crimes to another group, the target group of the hate crime is a minority member who in some way threatens the dominant group members. The key variable in reducing hate crimes that are caused by members of the dominant group is in simply showing them that the minority group members have much more in common with them, and that the perceived differences between the two groups is relatively insignificant.

(d) *Hate Crimes Occur within a "We-They" or "Us-Them" Dichotomy.* When we perceive others to be more similar to us, it becomes more difficult to not like them. In order for prejudice and ethnic conflict to develop, individuals first objectify and alienate the out-group by creating boundaries and distinctions. Once these boundaries have in fact become established, then it becomes easier for the dominant group members to discriminate against the minority group members. Once the discriminatory patterns have become established, then the minority group members begin to lose their perceived similarities in human qualities. They are not treated equally because they have become dehumanized and are now simply an inconvenience to the dominant group—more taxes, more competition for food, housing, etc.

People seem to naturally want to categorize things by way of classification and character. In some cases, individuals compare themselves with others by income, whereas in other situations the comparison may involve who has the more attractive house, front lawn or car. Perhaps one of the most fundamental and primitive forms of categorization with people involves our tendency to place others who are arbitrarily perceived more like us as the "we" or "us" group and those who are perceived in some way differently (ethnic differentiation, economic class, etc.) as the "they" or outside group. The "we-they" dichotomy refers to psychological phenomena where individuals must psychologically differentiate themselves from others in some way as being superior or somehow different in positive characteristics to the target group. Members in the "they" group or out-group categories have historically been viewed as having more negative characteristics and being less desirable in general than those who have been classified as the "us" (Oakes et al., 1994).

This differentiation therefore explains why those who do engage in hate crimes must first justify themselves as being somehow different (i.e., superior) than those members in the out-group. Conversely, the more we view others like ourselves as being in-group members, the less likely we are to act out aggressively towards them and engage in hate crimes. The more likely we can psychologically (and physically) create walls of differences between "them" and "us" the easier it is to engage in discrimination and hate crimes towards the minority or out-group member. The purpose of this chapter is in identifying those psychological techniques that contribute to the "we-they" dichotomy and identify strategies that encourage us to view all people as the "we" group.

If you assume that the vast majority of behaviors begin with our experiences in our environment, then hate crimes must develop first from some negative exposure in the environment. Certain reductionistic theorists, such as Freud, would argue that human behaviors are predestined to remain violent due to our human nature. However, we argue that hate crimes are learned through various negative experiences within our own environment. We should note that hate crimes involve different people in different age groups who *learn* to engage in harmful and aggressive behaviors towards other groups simply because of their identity within the group (religious, racial, gender). Note also that our emphasis is in *learning* hate crimes—individuals or groups of people must first *learn* how to engage in the destructive activity before it can occur.

Perhaps the most controversial of all topics addressing prejudice and discrimination is its origin—where exactly does it come from? If we were able to pinpoint the source of prejudice and discrimination, we would then have a much better ability to eliminate it in diverse populations. We have previously established in earlier chapters that human nature is not *ipso facto* racist or destructive in nature, but unfortunately a learned trait that needs to be examined in multicultural society.

In order for us to better understand the concepts and causal factors that are associated with hate crimes, we must first be able to describe what a hate crime is. A hate crime is described as any violent crime that is *intentionally directed* towards an individual (or group) based on the victim's gender, national origin, sexual identification, religion, or ethnicity. The key concept to note is intention — the crime must be intentionally directed to cause harm (either psychological or physical) in some way. Hate crimes target individuals who may be of minority ethnic descent or those who happen to differ from the dominant group in some way. Hate crimes may involve an individual's religion or they may also target those individuals who may suffer from some type of physical disability. Examples of current organizations that promote the philosophy of hate crimes would include the Ku Klux Klan or neo-Nazi groups.

It is disturbing to know that even young children are taught to separate and differentiate others by color or ethnicity, and that actions of violence towards these groups are rewarded. The rate of hate crimes has increased significantly over the last several years and unfortunately technology has aided in the development of hate websites. The Simon Wiesenthal Institute noted that in one year alone, hate crime websites increased from 163 in 1997 to 254 in 1998 (over 50 percent).

How Are Hate Crimes Learned?

The key factor in reducing and ultimately eliminating hate crimes altogether is first in identifying causal factors of why it exists. There are several theories that explain aggression in general, and to accurately describe hate crimes we need to first explore what are the general theories that influence aggression. The four most common theories describing hostility towards minority groups or hate crimes are the

a. Freudian instinct theory / drive hypothesis;
b. Albert Bandura's social learning theory;
c. Realistic conflict theory and
d. Miller and Dollard's (1939) frustration-aggression theory.

Freudian Instinct Theory

In this first theory of aggression that was originally proposed by Sigmund Freud (1929), all individuals are born with a biological drive or instinct towards aggression. According to Freud's theory, aggression is not a learned behavior, but something that we are all born with and that remains with us throughout our lifespan. It simply remains a part of our human nature and we need to find ways of dealing with it in more socially appropriate ways. Thus, we learn ways of dealing with people as a means of avoiding aggression, as violence and destruction according to Freud are natural and inevitable components of our personality. Interestingly, Freud indicated that watching violent movies or reading about similar types of literature does not increase our aggressive tendencies, but on the contrary reduces them through the process of a psychological phenomenon he referred to as catharsis. Catharsis is the psychological principle where we "work through" violent impulses by vicariously experiencing them through the media or some other accepted physical activity (i.e., a physical contact sport, such as football or boxing).

The aggressive instinct is within all of us and we are all capable of acting out destructively, as the famous poet and author Nietzsche notes, the "monster is within each of us." The "monster" in this case is the potential for all of us to engage in destruction and aggression against others. Human behaviors have historically fluctuated between the aggressive and destructive behaviors that we all know too well and the altruistic and good behaviors that are also possible. Freud argued that the destructive behaviors that were so common during his era (i.e., World Wars I and II) were an inevitable consequence of man's inhumanity to man. Where Darwin argues, "Biology is our destiny," Freud argues, "Anatomy is our destiny," meaning that ultimately what we want to do is of little consequence; it is the aggressive instinct that shapes our destiny. Freud was classified as a reductionist theorist, meaning that all of our human behaviors are ultimately reduced to aggressive instincts. "Humans," Freud argued, "cannot help themselves in their gradual and inevitable self-destruction." Clearly, this philosophy represents a belief that humans simply lack personal control and autonomy over their behaviors and ultimately are destined to their own destruction. This view is essentially fatalistic and does not take into consideration the many variables that exist within our environment that can shape and even promote positive and prosocial behaviors.

Perhaps a modernized view of the Freudian instinct theory may be what many psychologists now refer to as a "genetic predisposition" to behave a certain way. When people inherit genetic predispositions, the assumption today is that they have a genetic or inherent predisposition to behave a certain way (i.e., aggressively, or inclined towards substance abuse) and that some of their personal responsibility should be nullified because of the inherited predisposing factors.

When people are described as being "genetically predisposed" to behave a certain way, this means that they have inherited a genetic condition to behave in a particular manner. In Freud's case, he theorized that all individuals are predisposed to behave aggressively as it is part of our genetic constitution. As Darwin noted: "Biology is our Destiny"; so too would Freud agree that our biological constitution and genetic inheritance cause us to respond in aggressive manners. This does not mean that all people have to act out their aggression, but the instinct must be addressed in some way.

Catharsis — "Working Through" Inherited Aggressive Tendencies

Sigmund Freud argued that when individuals engage in catharsis, they are literally "working through" their aggression or hatred of other groups of people. Thus, an employee of a dominant group that works in a factory with other individuals of ethnic minority status would need to "redirect" (either psychologically or physically) his or her aggression towards specific members of minority groups. Freud argued that one reason why many individuals are so much attracted to aggression (i.e., watching violent movies or reading gratuitously violent material) is that these activities reduce our own tendency to engage in the violent activity itself.

Freud also described the process of catharsis as being achieved through physical activities (such as exercise) in that they would help reduce the tension and anxiety that ultimately would lead to aggression. Whether or not all humans are born with the instinct of aggression and that we are all predisposed to kill each other off remains highly controversial today. It is very easy to see how someone who is continuously exposed to violence on a daily basis (i.e., individuals living in a society where gang activity and crime is common) can believe that violence is a common instinct that we all share. When different ethnic groups all compete for increasingly limited resources, such as affordable housing, acceptance to prestigious colleges, or well paying jobs, often the result is conflict. We should not be surprised at Freud's interpretation of the universality of aggression, as he personally experienced and witnessed the imprisonment and ultimately the deaths of his three sisters during Hitler's regime in World War II and often experienced the anti-Semitism that was common throughout Europe during his lifetime.

Bandura's Social Learning Theory

We have described in previous chapters how behaviors may be learned from different sources and different types of environmental stimuli. Albert Bandura noted that when certain key figures (role models) display specific behaviors they are more likely to become imitated or emulated by other people, especially children (Bandura, 1969). If this theory is true, then it should be noted that children are highly susceptible to learning counterproductive and even aggressive behaviors towards ethnically diverse groups of individuals or any person who may appear to be physically different from them. Children learn aggressive behaviors and discriminatory behaviors from a variety of sources, but the role model who is portrayed in a positive and desirable manner has the most appeal to children and is thus most likely to be mimicked by them. Athletes, movies stars and modern-day heroes are all perceived as very positive role models and often children imitate their exact behaviors.

Teaching children cooperative behaviors and effective communication skills with a broad range of individuals from different environments and ethnic backgrounds is a great first step in helping children to appreciate and value diversity. Children are also very quick to observe, understand and incorporate subtle comments made by parents or older siblings that are offensive to other minority groups and imitate them as well. Exposure to these derogatory comments increases the likelihood of future discriminatory attitudes and they are also the foundation of hate crimes later in development (Bennett et al., 2004).

Realistic Conflict Theory as a Form of Institutionalized Racism

Increasingly we see in our society today competition for various resources—resources that include food, jobs, and housing. A common explanation why some ethnic groups are becoming targeted for specific types of hate crimes is that they are perceived as "taking away jobs" or resources from the dominant group. Is this claim truly justified, or is this an excuse to exhibit discrimination towards the minority group? Unfortunately, poor economic conditions can often lead to the dominant group engaging in blame and even aggression as a means of retaliation to the minority group for the economic recession.

A specific form of a hate crime can unfortunately manifest itself in many different types of environments and influence attitudes of many people. Gender, race, religion and sexuality are some of the most common targets of hate crimes. What makes hate crimes especially difficult to address is the seemingly positively influence it creates among individuals who have low self-esteem. When people criticize others based on ethnicity and use negative stereotypes, they are typically trying to make themselves feel better at the expense of the out-group. Additionally, when individuals engage in a specific form of a hate crime, others who condone the behavior typically reward them and this positive effect increases the likelihood of future hate crime activity. Individuals with a poor sense of self and low levels of self-esteem are likely to seek out environments that will enhance their ego and are driven to achieve approval from perceived authority figures. One effective method in reducing hate crimes is in educating individuals how to improve their own levels of self-efficacy and self-esteem without degrading minority groups or engaging in derogatory comments towards out-group members. Simply stated, individuals can learn to increase and improve their sense of self-esteem (i.e., cooperative group work) without criticizing other groups.

Frustration-Aggression Theory

In the frustration-aggression theory, Miller and Dollard (1939) argue that people do not possess biological "instincts" towards aggression as Freud would say, but rather, aggression is a natural and biological response when people are not able to achieve their short- or long-term goals. People typically become increasingly frustrated when their goals are continually blocked, such as a manager of a department store who applies for a promotion and year after year is rejected, or the doctoral candidate whose dissertation is rejected after years of work. The frustration-aggression theory explains why people suddenly snap and engage in some form of a violent or aggressive action, such as physical violence or hate crimes. Hate crimes are commonly associated with the frustration-aggression theory because the minority or out-group member is typically perceived as the cause of many problems and thus serves as the scapegoat for the economic and political problems in a given community. An employee who has been trying to achieve a promotion where he works may become frustrated and explode when a co-worker from the non-dominant group is awarded the promotion over him.

Affirmative action, immigration issues, employment and affordable housing are all very common examples today in our society where we see an increasing number of hate crimes directed towards members of the minority group. When people cannot acquire the standard of living that they feel that they are entitled to, their goals become consistently blocked and over time the likelihood for violence directed at the member of the minority group increases significantly. We see strong evidence in the relationship between the frustration-aggression theory and the existence of hate crimes when members of the dominant group become increasingly unable to achieve their goals.

For example, Conyers (2002) describes economically "lower class" whites as having more potential for holding prejudiced views as a means of maintaining "social order" and perceiving members of the out-group as threats to their ability to advance economically in a highly competitive employment field. Additionally, members of the dominant group that have limited economic resources are more likely to seek out other out-group members as the source of their limited income and most likely to respond negatively to assimilation measures, such as affirmative action and fair labor standards.

Addressing the Problem
of Hate Crimes: Change Is Possible

We have identified four key factors that have been identified as being associated and causing hate crimes:

a. Freud's instinctual theory, meaning all humans are in fact born with the drive and instincts that makes them predisposed to aggression;
b. Bandura's social learning theory, that describes aggression as a phenomenon that is learned through experiences in one's environment;
c. The realistic conflict theory; and
d. Miller and Dollard's key theory addressing the relationship between one's failure in achieving goals and increases in aggressive activities.

Perhaps most importantly, we now need to address methods that have been shown to reduce these hate crimes. In concluding our chapter, we will focus on three new strategies that have proven effectiveness in not only reducing ethnocentrism and hate crimes, but also can improve our relationships with each other.

3 Key Factors Necessary in Reducing Hate Crimes:

- Collaboration not competition—creating supportive environments;
- Increased interaction via community service work & interdependence;
- Rethinking your thoughts—cognitive revision;

Factors Causing Hate Crimes	*Factors Reducing Hate Crimes*
• Frustration-aggression (inability to achieve goals)	Group collaboration; interethnic community
• Social learning theory;	Service work; and
• Freud's instinctual theory	Cognitive revision

Can We Really Ever Stop Hate Crimes from Occurring? Analyze Your Own Opinion

A common question that I often ask my introductory psychology students is whether or not the existence of hate crimes can ever really be stopped. I also ask related questions, such as "Can groups of individuals live harmoniously without conflict or the need for police intervention?" or "Can a society live entirely cooperatively with each other?" A common theme on several reality television shows often portrays a group of selected volunteers to live together in an isolated environment and to try to rely on each other for survival. The conflict that members of the group have is in differentiating the needs of the self from the needs of the group. Only when members are able to make personal sacrifices to help the group are they ever typically capable of surviving in harsh environments. The same concept holds true among individuals living within a community and trying to achieve their personal goals. When all people work together for a common and mutually important goal, such as creating safe parks for children and clean urban environments, the outcome is usually successful.

In response to the question of living harmoniously without conflict, the answer is (theoretically) yes, but only if all people feel that these goals are achievable. Many people have different reactions to this question, with responses and reactions that range considerably. Some groups respond in disbelief as to how could I even think of such a question; others deliberate and think perhaps it could be possible. Perhaps most importantly, if we ever truly hope to address and ultimately reduce ethnocentric ideology and related hate crimes, it seems clear that a positive belief system exists that maintains we certainly can achieve our goals. Without first believing our goals are achievable, any effort to reduce hate crimes seems unrealistic.

While it may be unrealistic to expect all forms of aggression to simply just go away, it is critical to explore first our own attitudes towards the existence of a more tolerant and accepting society and culture if we truly wish to address the problem itself. If we maintain a negative view regarding hate crimes and aggression and believe (as Freud did) that they are ultimately inevitable, then this creates a type of a "self-fulfilling prophecy" where the hate crimes continue to develop. Making positive changes within our community starts with the simple philosophy in believing that positive changes can occur within the human personality. If we first do not believe that change is possible, then it will be very difficult to change other people's perceptions.

We certainly cannot expect the problems of aggression, hate crimes and ethnocentrism to diminish by themselves, and it would also certainly be naïve of us to believe that these problems will resolve themselves if first we ourselves do not believe this to be possible. We mention this psychological caveat now to help individuals realize that no theory is ever effective in addressing problems if people first do not believe in their validity and potential for change. *If we truly wish to see some forms of positive psychological and physical changes in our community, we first must believe that they in fact are achievable and that human nature is indeed capable of change.*

Perhaps the single most common factor that has been correlated with hate crimes involves competition and environments that require people to strive towards limited resources. Our first resource in eliminating hate crimes is in the transition from what is perceived as "competing environments" (i.e., jobs, school admissions, housing) to collaborative environments. We know that when people perceive others as competitors for a desirable outcome or goal (such as a high paying job), how they view others changes dramatically. In many situations, our economy may actually taint our perceptions of members from the out-group or minority groups, and in order to change this, our outlook on others must change from that of a "competitor" to one of a "supporter." We are much more likely to view others from different groups in a supportive way when we view them from a non-competitive perspective.

One of the most effective methods in eliminating competitive environments is through the modification of the environment itself. Instead of having singular or limited goals which can be achieved only by one person, we should focus more on creating goals that are capable of achievement by everyone. The development of what is referred to as superordinate or broad goals is a critical element that helps reduce group animosity and conflict because all members of the group are capable of achieving similar things cooperatively and collaboratively.

Muzafer Sherif (1966) conducted a classic study that describes how competition can create hostility among groups of boys between the ages of 9 through 12 years. In his classic study between "The Rattlers" and "The Eagles," Sherif was able to create highly competitive types of environments and situations among the boys that created hostility between the groups. In one situation the boys competed in a swimming contest against each other and were housed in separate camps away from each other. Sherif separated the boys from any type of cooperative mutual work and manipulated the environment where each group perceived the other as competing for various resources (i.e., food) and activities (i.e., contests).

The study was conducted in a traditional summer camp; within just a few days Sherif was able to create a highly hostile and antagonistic relationship between two groups of boys who prior to these events had either neutral or friendly relationships with one another. Sherif was able to reduce the animosity that had grown between the two groups of boys by creating artificial "helping situations" where both groups were required to work together. In one situation, for example, a truck had broken down that was taking both groups to the lake for a swimming activity. All of the boys had to get out of the truck and help fix the flat tire which promoted a sense of unity and togetherness that ultimately reduced the hostility that was evident between the groups just days earlier.

These results provide powerful evidence pointing to the effectiveness of group solidarity and cooperation as the single most effective tool in reducing not only ethnocentric attitudes and group conflict, but hate crimes that may be directed towards smaller out-groups. When individuals are provided with the opportunity to work together on mutual goals, they begin to see more similarities than differences, and this promotes ethnic cohesion and communication. More importantly, however, is the fact that through empirical research we have discovered highly effective methods to identify environments that are most likely to trigger hostility towards minority groups and that we can indeed change these behaviors first by recognizing their existence and engaging in cooperative styles of interaction. What Sherif and his colleagues were able to demonstrate was that change is possible when we emphasize common goals and mutual interests. When individuals (regardless of age) work towards a common goal, our attitudes towards that person (or group) improve significantly.

Increased Interaction via Community Service Work

A second highly effective method in addressing and reducing hate crimes is a topic that we have frequently mentioned in this text—community service work. The primary advantage of community service work relative to interethnic group relations is that it is an activity that allows all groups of individuals to work cooperatively with each other in the development of a necessary goal that is shared by all people. Numerous studies in research show that when people work together for a common goal, their attitudes towards each other significantly improve. The previous study mentioned in this chapter by Sherif (1965) demonstrated that groups of young boys who work cooperatively on a mutual task would improve their relationships with each other significantly. Working on mutual tasks helps us to diminish perceived differences and allows us to focus on what we have in common with each other. This positive sense of cooperative behavior is vital among ethnically diverse communities, where it has become easy to see differences and antagonism develops quickly. When environments become non-competitive and focus on mutual goals, positive relationships emerge within diverse groups and increase the likelihood of future cooperative work in the future.

Rethinking Your Thoughts— Cognitive Revision Theory

Our final recommendation in addressing and reducing hate crimes is in how we think about important things in our lives. Often our thoughts influence our behaviors, so it remains logical that in order to influence or to change negative behaviors, we must first change our thoughts. There have been many different types of cognitive psychologists who have described highly effective methods in identifying the relationship between attitudes, thoughts and cognitive belief systems with success in behavioral change. In order to first make something happen, it is necessary to first believe it to be possible to happen. Cognitive revision means simply to change how we think about individuals and members from specific groups. Often discrimination, prejudice and hate crimes are motivated and charged by incorrect or faulty styles of thinking. Stereotypes, for example, feed into a faulty belief system (prejudice) that often leads to discriminatory behaviors and then can influence the discrimination into hate crimes.

The formula for the development of hate crimes first includes differences in the styles of interaction among groups—people who engage in hate crimes feel anger that is directed towards the minority group usually for some specific reason. When our cognitive affect remains positive we are more likely to encounter positive experiences with those around us (Mayer & Hanson, 1995). One important method that may reduce ethnic conflict is in maintaining positive affects among individuals who frequently interact with diverse groups. If your current mood remains positive throughout the day you are more likely to engage in positive and rewarding interactions with individuals of different ethnic or economic backgrounds and even experience different environments more positively.

An additional point to consider is the relationship between mood, affect and cognition. The more likely individuals are capable of monitoring and controlling their emotions, the more likely they are to experience positive relationships with others (Tykocinski, 2001). Thus, imagine the ramifications of our work in improving race relations and reducing ethnocentrism — if individuals can control negative affect when interacting among ethnically diverse groups, they will be significantly more likely to experience positive emotions and reduce ethnocentric attitudes.

Changing Thoughts
Can Change Attitudes

The famous cognitive therapist Aaron Beck argued that in many cases irrational belief systems play a role in dominating unhealthy and counterproductive behaviors. One very basic and yet highly successful cognitive technique that is used to reduce prejudice and ethnocentric behaviors is what Beck refers to as the "Just Saying No" technique. In cognitive therapy, individuals are provided with instructions to think "positive thoughts" to help them in redirecting negative thoughts into positive behaviors that affect their personal lives, their professional environment and their relationships with others. Beck maintains that often we tell ourselves things that "must be true" and often can lead to depression. Examples of these irrational thoughts may include:

- "Everyone must like or love who I am and I must be accepted by all people."
- "If I do not get my job promotion or raise then I am a failure."
- "My group is inherently better than other groups."

Beck further argues that these irrational behaviors can contribute to some of the most common problems among groups of people, including depression, anxiety and (for our purposes) prejudice and ethnocentrism. In cognitive revision theory, individuals who engage in the counterproductive or irrational thoughts are instructed to think positive and rational thoughts. With positive and rational statements about the self, the individual will experience higher levels of self-esteem and self-efficacy and thus feel less compelled to criticize others based on race or ethnicity. Common positive statements about the self that are used to improve self-esteem or self-efficacy may include:

- "I'm getting better at achieving my goals."
- "I am capable of learning and changing just like other people."
- "I have self-worth and value and can interact and communicate with others who will appreciate me."

Some of the more specific cognitive thoughts that may help reduce prejudice may include what Beck (1993) calls "thought stopping" techniques. In the practice of thought stopping, the individual is instructed to stop thinking negative thoughts and to counter with positive thoughts about a particular situation or person. For example, assume an individual is thinking about joining a group in school to complete and academic assignment. The group consists of Hispanic and African American students. The negative thought might include: "They look different from me.... I want to work with people who are more like me." In cognitive revision theory, the student would be instructed to think the following: "The students in the group are different from me, but we might work better on the assignment by comparing our ideas and thoughts together. It might be a very good educational experience to get to know people who are different from me and develop new friendships."

In cognitive revision theory, individuals are instructed to change how they think about the target group and to shift their negative thoughts into positive thoughts. Additionally, the negative thoughts that are associated with the minority group are often based on stereotypes that have proven to be inaccurate or false (Kawakami, 2000). In a clever study conducted by Kawakami, subjects were shown pictures of Caucasian (dominant) groups and African American (non-domi-nant) groups. Subjects were instructed to associate stereotypical phrases with different ethnic groups and their reaction times were recorded. Kawakami theorized that if sub-jects engaged in cogni-tive rehearsal training that was supposed to debunk the negative stereotype, then the reaction times of the photos of the ethnic groups with stereotyp-ical statements would be significantly reduced.

Prejudice

↓

(Thinking one individual is inferior to the others);

Ethnocentrism

↓

(A belief system that one's own ethnic group is superior to others);

Discrimination

↓

(Exclusionary actions based on prejudicial thoughts);

Hate Crimes

↓

(Intentional harm or destruction committed to the minority group)

The results were very significant in the sense that subjects in the experi-mental group took significantly more time to associate one group (dom-inant group versus the minority group) with common stereotypes. Thus, cognitive rehearsal training skills such as the cognitive revision theory may actually help us to reduce negative stereotypes that have been asso-ciated with the minority group.

Some of the more common misperceptions that fuel hate crimes include:

• "The minority group is taking something away that belongs to me (i.e., property, jobs, income, etc.), that belongs to my group."

- "The minority group is threatening the social, educational or moral development of my group, my children, my family."
- "The minority group is inherently different from my group."

Often, a pattern of thinking that becomes biased begins in the following way (see figure 11c) that can lead to ethnic conflict and hate crimes. After reviewing figure 11c, take the ATIQ (Attitudes towards Immigration Questionnaire) survey and see how your attitudes reflect the topics of immigration, acculturation and assimilation of new ethnic groups.

12

The Critical Periods for Incorporating Community Service Work Principles

Often when adults try to learn new or different types of behavior, they comment that things were much easier to learn when they were younger and that they were even more likely to learn things faster in their youth. While many older individuals wax about their youthful days, we need to remember that the capacity to change our attitudes and behaviors can occur *anytime* as long as we are ready to make the commitment for change. However, it is also true that many attitudes (negative or positive) addressing race and ethnicity over time become more difficult to change due to the development and resistance of stereotypes.

Perhaps what these individuals really are referring to is a limited period of time where learning occurs most efficiently and is retained for indefinite periods of time. Imagine, for example, trying to learn how to ride a bicycle for the first time or learn how to swim as an adult. Imagine trying to learn a second or third language as an adult. Most adults feel that these cognitive skills and behaviors are significantly more difficult (but not impossible) to learn later in adult life, and they usually regret that they were not first learned as a child.

The terms "critical period" or "sensitive period" are concepts that are commonly used in developmental psychology to describe a limited opportunity of time to learn a particular behavior or cognitive skill. Social psychologists have long known that learning certain critical features that are unique to human behaviors (i.e., language development) often are learned best during limited windows of time (Hess & Petrovich, 1977). Researchers have long known that certain cognitive skills and physical behaviors can be taught and learned more readily at specific ages of development (Au, Knightly, Jun & Oh, 2002; Bavelier, Newport, & Supalla,

167

2003). For example, teaching children a second or third language is most readily developed when they are very young infants, from six months of age to ages three or four years. Similarly, if infants lack cognitive stimulation and interaction with adults in their environment, their ability to process new information becomes limited (Brace, Morton, & Munakata, 2006).

How are the concepts of interethnic activities and critical periods related to community service work? Perhaps it may very well be possible (just as in languages) to teach children and adults the value and benefits of community service work that may be readily incorporated into different aspects of their psychosocial development. Researchers are aware, for example, that children who are taught the value and importance of physical exercise are more likely to continue exercising as adults. Additionally, when parents become involved in the activity then children are most likely to incorporate the activity on a regular basis. We maintain the parental relationship in teaching children the value and importance of community service work is vital if it is going to continue on into adulthood.

Once incorporated, community service work can continue to play a vital and instrumental role in fulfilling service and meaning to the individual's life. Furthermore, once interethnic community service learning principles have been established, we hypothesize that problems relative to ethnically diverse communities, such as prejudice and discrimination, will be significantly reduced. Additionally, we hypothesize that community service work activities are most likely to continue throughout the lifespan once they have been established in early development.

The primary theme of this chapter is in describing how the fundamental principles of community service work may be taught to people in different age groups throughout the lifespan. More importantly, however, is the critical element of not only just implementing community service learning principles at various points of development in one's life, but how community service work can provide meaning, integrity and purpose within the person who is involved in these principles. Many stage theorists and psychologists argue that perhaps the most critical element of personal happiness in one's life is in having the opportunity to participate in meaningful group activities with others, helping others, and, through our community service involvement, seeing a purpose and meaning to our own existence. An additional theme of this chapter is in describing how interethnic community service activities will help promote communication among ethnically diverse groups and reduce prejudice and discrimination in our communities.

In psychological theory, critical periods are very important concepts that can have a profound influence in various types of social and educational experiences. Additionally, critical periods are important in the sense that they not only allow us to become more adaptive in learning key behaviors, but also they are necessary factors in the development of healthy cognitive growth and stimulation. Traditionally in psychology, the concept of "critical periods" has been reserved for various forms of cognitive skills, such as language development and math skills. When children have reached the age of 8 months to one year, they typically begin to experiment in speaking their first words. Infants are not just capable of learning to speak languages during their first few years of life, but for adequate cognitive development they *must* to be exposed to languages. If an infant is not exposed to any form of cognitive stimulation relative to languages, infants lose their capacity to speak languages later in development.

In this chapter we propose a new concept relative to the use of the term "critical period." We argue that the topic of community service work may in fact become more readily developed and understood in specific and early chronological stages of development. We further argue that a critical period exists not only for various forms of cognitive information (such as languages) but also in psychosocial development, such as the development of basic community service skills and behaviors. Additionally, in this chapter we propose that individuals (adults as well as children) periodically encounter various age-related episodes in their lives where community service work plays a critical role in establishing meaning and purpose within the context of their personal and professional lives. These three critical areas where community service learning principles may become vital in establishing meaning and purpose would include early childhood experiences, the classic midlife crisis during middle adulthood, and finally late adulthood and helping older adults establish integrity and meaning as they mature.

While community service work is a valuable experience at any age, we describe the principles of this special form of volunteer work as being highly sensitive or critical to specific stages of human development. Community service work is most influential and positive when experienced at three critical phases of development. In early childhood, young children need to not only learn the value of sharing work responsibilities, they can also gain tremendous value in learning to work with others who may be different in appearance to them (i.e., interethnic activities). Early exposure to ethnically diverse populations can improve how we interact with others as adults and reduce the likelihood for prejudice and discrimination (Martin & Nakayama, 2004). In middle adulthood, community service work can provide meaning to one's life that appears to have become "stagnant" by an overreliance on materialistic possessions, commonly referred to as "conspicuous consumerism." Community service activities during this period of time takes the emphasis off the individual ("It's all about me") and replaces egoism with community service responsibility in helping others. During this traditional midlife crisis, adults realize that meaning can often come in the service of helping others. Finally, and perhaps most importantly, community service work is critical in late adulthood as a means of maintaining integrity and genuine meaning in our lives through activities with other lives.

We propose the following three dominant psychosocial themes of development are readily available for incorporating and learning community service work principles: Early childhood (ages 3–6 years); middle adulthood (ages 40–65 years) and late adulthood (age 65 and beyond):

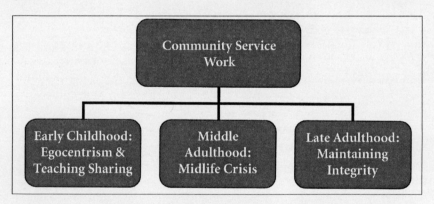

Early Childhood (3 to 6 years)

One of the most important features of childhood is in the development interactive social skills. A dominant and problematic feature of early childhood is that of egocentrism–the child's belief that his or her needs are most important combined with an inability or reluctance to consider other people's views, feelings or thoughts. A challenge for all young children is in learning to delay their needs and to recognize the needs of others and to share cooperatively with their peers. If children are not exposed to environments that promote selfless and cooperative behaviors, they will develop a self-entitlement orientation in their relationship with others.

They will also have difficulty in understanding different perspectives other than their own.

A highly egocentric child will soon develop into a highly egocentric adolescent if he or she is not first taught the value and importance of the principles of sharing, cooperative behaviors, and considering the views of others. Community service work is a highly effective tool in counteracting the negative impact of egocentrism because the central focus of community service work is directed towards the community itself. Teaching community service work as a means of helping others and learning to emerge from childhood egocentrism is an essential skill in establishing positive relationships with others, especially later in development. Teaching the principles of community service work and allowing children to engage in the activities involving community service work are excellent opportunities for them to learn how to share and appreciate differences in thinking and problem-solving activities. In our community service gardening work, students were able to engage in a community improvement project and share their ideas on how to develop and maintain a vegetable garden. That activity required them to solve problems together and to communicate with others who have had significantly different backgrounds and experiences than they may have had. In short, the community service activities provided the students with an opportunity to see how life is in very different perspectives and helped them to debunk some of the negative stereotypes that they may have had prior to the activities they were involved with.

Organizing interethnic recreational and educational activities can significantly reduce overt prejudice and increase communication among ethnically diverse groups. We maintain that ethnic conflict is a result of learned behaviors and economic factors that often make ethnically diverse populations targets of prejudice, discrimination and hate crimes. By teaching children the principles of community service work, children are not only learning how to engage in community projects to improve their environment, they also learn how to engage in interethnic activities that will reduce ethnic polarization and prejudice later in development. Children can also be taught to participate in cooperative tasks that include other children from different ethnic groups.

Exposure to ethnically diverse groups of other children allow for opportunities to share experiences that help them to discover similarities (and differences regarding several activities and projects). Eliot Aronson has embarked on a project that he calls the jigsaw classroom that allows all students from different backgrounds to pull together to complete a variety of different types of academic projects. The jigsaw classroom projects typically assign one project to several interethnic groups and students must devise a plan to complete the project where each member contributes to the solution to the problem. When ethnically diverse groups of young children learn to cooperate with each other on academic tasks, their ability to work cooperatively as adults in interethnic populations is vastly improved and more evident (Slavin, 1989).

The Crisis of Early Childhood: Learning to Share or Self-Entitlement?

Often researchers in early childhood discuss the need for young children to learn to share and to interact with other children as a means of overcoming their egocentric tendencies. Community service work is an ideal activity to teach young children because it provides them with an opportunity to learn how to engage in constructive activities that are designed to improve a variety of public environments. Community service work is also a valuable experience that shows children the value and importance in volunteering their time and effort to improve their community and to work collaboratively with others. Community service work shows children how communities need to have everyone share in the responsibility in maintaining public areas.

When children are not afforded the opportunity to work cooperatively with others (i.e., friends or siblings), they tend to engage in more egoistic behaviors and become more self-oriented (Dunn, 1992). Additionally, children who lack interactive activities and socialization skills with other children tend to experience more problems in social interaction and even more victimized by aggression from other children (Kitzmann, Cohen & Lockwood, 2002). These types of behaviors are very common within our culture (the individualistic culture) where we emphasize independence and individualism and winning at any cost. Without community service work, younger children lack the opportunities to see how volunteer work can not only improve the community, but also improve our relationships with others regardless of socioeconomic status or ethnicity.

A related issue that is commonly associated with egoistic behaviors is the self-entitlement culture that commonly found in individualistic cultures. A common problem that is associated with environments that lack community service work opportunities is an increase in the culture of self-entitlement. Whereas the principles of community service work teach children the value and benefits of volunteering their time and work towards the community, the concept of self-entitlement is entirely different. In the self-entitlement culture, individuals expect others to do things for them and do not engage in any type of volunteer activity. Self-entitlement literally is the antithesis of community service work because of the lack of individual responsibility to engage in any type of volunteer work that is designed to improve society or community (Hoffman & Wallach, 2007c). Self-entitlement is essentially an egoistic view of the world where an "ends justify the means" perspective influences individual behaviors and legitimizes selfish and self-oriented behaviors. Cultures that fail to teach the value and benefits of community service work to children are creating future environments that are prone to self-oriented and even hostile behaviors among future generations.

A child that is not exposed to the dynamic principles of community service work is missing the valuable opportunities in communicating, collaborating and sharing in valuable group activities. These group activities may benefit him or her in many ways later in development relative to interaction with peers and socialization skills. Community service work helps benefit children in four key ways: education, community engagement, psychosocial skills, and physical health:

Educational Benefits

Children learn through interactive participation in various community service activities. Children learn how to cooperate and share responsibilities in a variety of academic and educational projects, creating educational or academic group assignments where children take turns being the group leader. The educational projects should be directed towards some activity designed for campus involvement (i.e., "school improvement day"), such as schools hosting other schools, giving students from different backgrounds opportunities to meet and work with each other. Each student shares and contributes information to the group. At the end of the project, students write down the information that they feel is most valuable.

Community Engagement

Creating recreational community service activities where children work under the supervision of adults. Community engagement activities can help establish a sense of social responsibility for older children and adolescents. Sample activities include planting trees and flowers in public parks to improve a community area or picking up trash to improve a public park. These activities will help not only improve public areas but will also allow for children to increase their health through physical outdoor activities, such as increases in walking, hiking, bending, lifting, and so on.

Physical Health Benefits

Because of its inherently active and dynamic nature, community service activities help people not only to remain more physically active, but also can help us to lose weight. Consider the following:

• Approximately 65 percent of adults living in the United States are overweight;
• Almost 20 percent of children between ages 2 to 19 are overweight;
• Less than one-third of young people in grades 9–12 get enough physical exercise;
• Over 43 percent of adolescents watch over 2 hours of television daily (*The Daily News*, November 19, 2007).

Psychosocial Benefits

Exposing children to a variety of community service activities helps them to establish personal responsibility in carrying out tasks as well as improving self-esteem and academic self-efficacy (Hoffman, 2006).

These sobering statistics should serve as a reminder that community service activity can help to counteract the increasingly negative consequences of a sedentary society. When you are involved in a community activity that is designed to help others, you are typically very active. The greatest contributor to obesity (contrary to what many people think) is not particularly diet or calories, but more importantly how active (or sedentary) a person is.

Middle Adulthood:
Achieve Meaning by Giving
Back to the Community

Many psychosocial theorists and researchers have described middle adulthood as one of the most problematic stages of development for several reasons. Middle adulthood is typically a period of time where many people feel that they have "reached their peak" and they often compare themselves to others as a gauge of success or failure. Often, the person who "owns the most toys" is the most successful by virtue of economic success. However, this is precisely the problem or "crisis" that is associated with this period of development. Too much reliance on possessions or things as a means of providing us with meaning in our lives often comes with a profound sense of emptiness and stagnation. Things get old and wear out soon; investments in the relationships with people may last a lifetime. The commonly cited midlife crisis essentially represents a critical appraisal of our own life. The midlife crisis becomes a transition in which we gain meaning in our lives through qualitative experiences with others and shift from our needs to the needs of others in our community. Additionally, the midlife crisis represents choice that people can make regarding how meaning is achieved in their lives— either through ownership of possessions or experiencing meaning by giving back to others via community service work.

When we use money, financial gain or possessions as the sole criteria for happiness and success in our life, we are destined to experience a painful void — what Erikson (1963) refers to as "stagnation." The key in maintaining happiness and meaning in one's life, especially during the midlife period, is through the context of our relationships with others. More specifically, meaning is only achieved during this traumatic period of midlife development when we are provided with opportunities to "give back" essential skills that we have developed over the course of our lives. Community service work provides the perfect forum in maintaining meaning and purpose during this turbulent phase of adult development because it clarifies our role with others and gives purpose and meaning to our existence.

The period of middle adulthood is a time when most adults have expectations of "something more" in their lives. The crisis is developed when we become preoccupied with our own needs, our own happiness (often at the expense of others) and a type of self-absorption develops that is all too common in the western individualistic culture. Furthermore, during the midlife phase, we often begin to develop unrealistic expectations in terms of what kinds of things are most likely to make us happy. We tend to rely more on things (i.e., money) rather than relationships and communications as viable sources of happiness and meaning. These expectations may come in the form of income or money, possessions, or just an expectation of being in a different place in their lives. Often the middle adulthood stage brings with it a sense of ennui or malaise where there is a comparison with others who appear to be better off than we are. Many psychosocial theorists and psychologists argue that a midlife crisis is really more about experiencing a psychological rut or boredom with one's life. Furthermore, individuals at this phase of their life often ask themselves if this is all there is to life and have a generalized feeling of emptiness and boredom.

Community Service Work in Middle Adulthood: The Cure for the Midlife Crisis

Community service work allows opportunities for adults to provide what they have learned in their lives to younger people so they may benefit from their experiences. A common problem that is experienced among middle-aged adults is a sense of void or meaninglessness that is typically a result of an overreliance on materialistic possessions to provide meaning to their lives. Several researchers have identified a basic need that many middle-aged adults have to "give back" some of their knowledge and experiences to younger people. The process and experience of giving back to others automatically provides a true sense of meaning and purpose in one's life (Erikson, 1963).

Community service work provides individuals with opportunities to give back the knowledge and experiences that they have gained over the years. The interaction that is gained by teaching younger persons key experiences that will help them in their future typically plays a vital role in establishing meaning in the life of the adult. Community service work is a wonderful opportunity that allows individuals to work with others in a variety of community tasks where they are able to share their knowledge with other persons and develop positive relationships with others in the process. Samples of community service work that is available for midlife adults include working with children in a community gardening program, volunteer coaching at local recreational parks, or helping as a volunteer in community clinics and hospitals. As long as there is a need for experienced mentors to help others, there will be a need for community service work.

Perhaps part of the reason why the midlife crisis is common among middle-aged adults is a cultural phenomenon. Living within the individualistic culture (i.e., more of a focus on individual needs without concern over the group) we tend to place more of an emphasis on our own needs and neglect the larger group. In collectivistic cultures (i.e., typically Asia), the midlife crisis is virtually nonexistent, as meaningful experiences are obtained during middle adulthood by contributing and giving back to the group, with less emphasis on individual competition and more of a focus on group development. Meaning relative to one's life and accomplishments are placed within the context of our relationship to the group itself; belonging to the group as well as making personal contributions to the group is the defining feature in maintaining meaning and purpose in one's life. Within the collectivistic culture, the identity of the individual is achieved first through identity with the group itself.

Alfred Adler and Community Service Work: "The Psychic Life of Man Is Determined by His Goals and Relation to the Community"

The principles of community service work are certainly not new, but the increasingly important need for contribution to the mission of community service work is becoming more relevant today. Early research into the works of ego psychoanalyst Alfred Adler addresses the critical need of the individual to identify with the group and to be provided with opportunities to contribute to the needs of the community. Community service work and volunteer behaviors, by definition, are collectivistic because of the emphasis on group identity and interdependency. Meaningful activities to the group provide meaning to the individual as well as a source of identity. Community service work and volunteer work that is designed to help others who belong to the community help us to focus on maintaining purpose and meaning in our own lives by helping others with their lives. In much of Alfred Adler's research addressing social creativity and contribution to society, he describes how individuals need to provide for others within the community as a vital characteristic in maintaining meaning in their own lives, a concept that he coined as *Gemeinschaftsgefühl*— the individual need of all persons to contribute to the community for a sense of "wholeness," solidarity or completeness (Adler, 1927).

Theorists such as Adler, Abraham Maslow and even Charles Darwin argued that a primary and basic experience that is central in human nature is in participating in the experience of sharing and contributing to the welfare of others. Adler argues that a sense of community is necessary to bring out the individual strengths and aptitudes that all persons innately possess. Maslow argues that all persons are driven to improve or self-actualize themselves through a series of motivational hierarchies. Each hierarchy is distinguished by the compelling need to make increasingly sacrificial behaviors in improving the human condition — trend from early egoistic needs to the ultimate altruistic actions that define the greatest virtues in human behaviors.

Even Charles Darwin (not known for attributing particularly humanistic characteristics to human nature) commented on the "weakness" of human nature and the necessity of the division of labor and cooperation for the survival of the species as being central to the qualities of human behavior. When we are capable of providing something that is critical and of value to others, we develop and maintain meaning within our own lives. Thus, humans are essentially social and interactive creatures that need various opportunities to develop and share their skills with others. Without opportunities that are similar to community service work and volunteer work in our society, people would essentially lead unfulfilled lives that lack meaning and passion. The primary message that the humanistic theorists offer is that human behavior is essentially positive and community oriented; in this regard, then, communities have an obligation to link the skills of the individual with the needs of the society at large. Individuals do not fail societies, but rather societies often fail the individual in their lack of opportunities for engagement.

We can summarize the midlife crisis into four distinct stages:

- Self-Oriented Phase & "It's All About Me": Early midlife adults are concerned primarily with getting ahead in their lives and conspicuous consumption, where their philosophy of "more is better even at the cost of others" influences their context of relationships with people. Possessions and ownership of things are the capstone markers of success and midlife adults tend to take for granted their relationships with people and family. Typically this is a period of self-absorption and entitlement for many adults.
- Shallowness Phase: Midlife adults are typically preoccupied with income and excessive ownership of things which are used as a gauge for success. Typically there is a lack of meaning in one's life based on the expectation of things providing intrinsic meaning in one's life rather than people. Excessive reliance on materialistic possessions typically yields an unhappy and empty experience. As time progresses during the midlife

phase, preoccupation with materialistic possessions soon gives way to shallowness and a sense of unfulfilled dreams. Midlife adults also now begin to realize that they will eventually be unsuccessful in achieving all of their dreams. Questions that are often raised at this midlife crisis include: "Is this all that there is in my life?"

- Reassessment of Personal Values. The third phase of the midlife crisis involves a *reassessment* of the value of people and relationships with others as a primary and meaningful experience in one's life. Meaning is essentially achieved through giving to others and making sacrifices for others.
- Community Service Work Discovery: The midlife adult discovers now that meaning is achieved through giving to others and helping to improve the human condition by making personal sacrifices for others. Meaning and purpose is now achieved not through ownership of things but more through the context of our relationship with others and providing assistance to build communities (see figure 12b below).

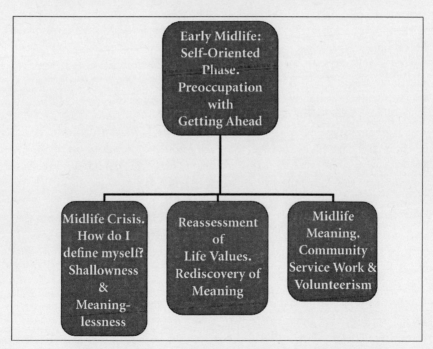

Late Adulthood:
Achieving Integrity

Perhaps historically the most challenging of all crises that we face throughout our life development is that of late adulthood. Our health typically begins to deteriorate, our social network changes where we find more of our friends and family members dying off, and typically our financial support systems also become strained. We physically cannot do the things that we once did, and we often become more dependent on others for the basic things in our lives, such as transportation and food. Costs relative to medical care and health begin to take their toll, and our choices at this final stage of development appear quite limited. Life can be very difficult — but we can still maintain and even enhance some levels of integrity and happiness if we incorporate community service work principles during this final stage of development. At this phase of development, the older adult must come to recognize his or her limitations (physical and cognitive) and yet somehow must define their integrity within their lifespan. Here the individual reflects and identifies the variables that provide meaning in his or her life, despite the increasing limitations that come with late adulthood. Here Erikson describes the primary challenge as being one of maintaining a sense of integrity and purpose in one's life, even though we face tremendous obstacles and physical limitations as we progress into our seventh, eighth and ninth decades.

The final stage of psychosocial development is most difficult because of the many challenges that face the older adult: What does one have to look forward to if they face terminal illness? How can the older adult still develop and maintain integrity if they are entirely dependent on others to help? The challenge facing the older adult is in facing all of these limitations relative to health and income and still maintaining self-respect and integrity within their lives. *The key component in helping older adults achieve integrity in their final stage is not showing what others can do for them, but integrity and meaning is achieved in showing the older adult what they can still do for others.*

What makes this last stage of development most unique is in the social network that once existed for older adults. The "social network" refers to the network of family and friends that are used as important support systems and emotional support throughout the adult person's life. For example, by the time older adults reach the age of 85, over 60 percent of males and 42 percent of females have experienced a loss by a family member or friend within the last year (Johnson & Troll, 1991).

The experience of losing family and friends at such a frequent pace (typically without replacement) is typically very stressful. Community service work can be a very effective activity to help older adults deal with the loss of their friends and family by placing them in various types of new environments (such as hospitals, schools, self-help programs, etc.) and provide them with opportunities to re-connect with people and their communities. Often when older adults simply have a place to go or if they feel that they are needed in some way, these are the critical differences in maintaining a life that has meaning and integrity.

What are the specific ways community service work projects can help older adults maintain meaning and integrity within their lives? How can community service activities still promote integrity and meaning as one matures into late adulthood?

Prioritizing Choices

A very common concern among many older adults is loss of autonomy and independence as they mature and become older. Many individuals in this stage of life fear a life of dependency on others in daily necessary activities, such as shopping for food, bathing and grooming. Research has shown consistently that when older adults remain engaged in a variety of activities, such as community service work and volunteer work, the negative side effects that are commonly associated with aging are postponed and delayed. Older adults who participate in a variety of community service projects are actually able to maintain their independence longer and can actually live healthier and more productive lifestyles while providing service to others.

Older adults now focus more on what they *can* do at this stage rather than what they *cannot* do. Community service activities allow older adults to prioritize their activities and choose how they wish to spend their time in helping others. Older adults who can make choices in how they wish to engage in activities are typically happier because they are still capable of making positive decisions in their lives. Older adults are also happier when they can actively seek out different types of community service programs that provide meaning in their lives. Older adults need to remain active in what they can do and resourceful in the things that they cannot do. In an age where older adults have fewer and fewer choices due to physical limitations, community service work provides older adults with a proactive method to continue to find meaning and integrity within their lives. Previously we mentioned that the older adult's social network (i.e., friends and family members that provide love and support) may have diminished. This may be true, but proactive participation in community service work will allow the older adult to reestablish new friendships and thus create a new social network. A key element to successful and happy transition into late adulthood is adaptiveness and responding positively to new changes in the older adult's lifestyle. Simply having a need and purpose to wake up each day is critical in maintaining integrity in the older adult life. Community service activities, such as volunteer coaching with children at a local park or even maintaining a community garden are excellent methods in fostering meaning in one's life. For example, knowing that children rely on you to help organize a baseball game may provide meaning in your life if only for a limited period of time. Knowing that plants and vegetables may perish if you are not available to maintain and water them is another excellent example of how community service activities may foster meaning in one's life. Other examples of viable community service work include volunteering at local hospitals, daycare facilities, or parks and recreation services for children and youth.

Prioritizing Time

As we age our experiences in how we value time changes considerably (Bruno, 1997). Older persons frequently comment that their time seems to pass at a faster and faster pace. Time remains constant, but our subjective experiences that are associated with chronological age change with time. Prioritizing time means realizing that our time is limited and we need to make important decisions in choosing how our time is spent with others. What seemed for an eternity as a child (i.e., one hour) now perhaps flashes by in an instant in the world of the older adult. Because our perceptions of time change with age, we need to plan our activities more carefully as we mature and develop into late adulthood. Now more than ever, older adults need to prioritize (i.e., schedule) their time. Instead of allowing older adults to "burn time away" community service activities provide older adults with a variety of ways to continue to find meaning. Individuals who are actively involved with community service activities have difficulty in doing all of the things they want to do—rarely do they experience boredom or a sense of a "loss of purpose." Community service work and volunteer work are important methods where older adults can make valuable use of their time and make positive contributions at the same time. This can be achieved by planning out daily activities and engaging in structured community activities that provide opportunities for engagement with friends and members of the community.

Prioritizing Health

Finally, late adulthood is often associated with physical limitations. While it is true older adults lose some of their mobility, community service work helps keep older adults fit and active by increasing their physical movement. For example, 45 minutes of gardening can be very challenging, and older adults who are involved in park programs involving exercise or gardening programs can benefit tremendously. Having a sense of purpose combined with a program designed to increase physical activities are two of the most critical things that older persons can do to improve their overall quality of living. Community service activity programs can actually help to maintain physical health because they involve movement and physical activities—cleaning up parks, planting flowers, or growing vegetables in a community garden help to keep older adults active but more importantly provides them with a sense of purpose that is critical to their lives. Community service work helps older adults with both a sense of purpose in sharing time with others to improve their lives and maintaining activity levels to improve their physical health. Samples of community physical activity programs for the older adult include:

- Power walking for 30 to 60 minutes. The walking activities are ideal for older adults who are mobile and will help them to appreciate outdoor activities as well as improve their health.
- Light to moderate gardening activities. The gardening activities may be designed to improve a public community area, such as parks and recreational facilities. For example, older adults may organize a community gardening program and help distribute the produce to the needy in low-income areas. One highly successful program at Compton Community College is called "GROVE" (Growing Real, Organic Vegetables Everyday). The older community residents take a proactive role in not only preparing the garden for the community, but they also distribute the vegetables and plants to the community members. The Compton community older adults take a very proactive role in preparing the vegetable gardens and this community service work has provided them with a very real and unique sense of purpose to their lives.

• Volunteer services at children's centers, daycare centers, or hospitals. As we have mentioned previously, in late adulthood it is critical that older adults maintain a sense of meaning and purpose in their lives by participating in any activity where they can contribute and enjoy. Simply knowing that people, animals and even plants depend on you for their well-being can be highly therapeutic in an environment and culture that so quickly discards the value and wisdom of late adulthood.

Change Is Possible!

Our primary intention in writing this text was in describing to you the vast and dynamic importance of community service work relative to interethnic groups living together. Central to this point is the key topic of *interdependency* — the psychological positive experience of providing and sharing something of value possessed by the individual to the overall welfare of the group itself. We have identified several ideas and theories describing how hate crimes and ethnic violence develop in society today. Our last (cognitive) point is perhaps the most important relative to our theories in addressing race relation: *we all have the capacity to make rational and positive choices in our lives that ultimately improve our relationships with others.*

A frequent reminder that is critical in making change possible is first in believing that change can and will occur. Without this critical belief system, changes in negative stereotypes towards various ethnic groups will never occur. We raise this critical point at the conclusion of our text because so many persons (unfortunately) believe that destructive behaviors such as hate crimes, prejudice and ethnic conflict are inevitable. They are not inevitable as long as people are considered to be rational creatures capable of making sound decisions in their lives. In order to answer this question, one must first determine his or her views determining human nature itself. Clearly, reductionistic theorists such as Freud, Darwin or Nietszche would argue that biology is our destiny and we lack the ability to live cooperatively. Additionally, these theorists and philosophers would lead us to believe that without the existence of laws in society anarchy would ultimately and inevitably follow. Individuals who believe that human nature is destined to self-destruction and conflict have little hope in believing that interethnic conflict, prejudice and hate crimes will ever become reduced or minimized in our society. Thus, the first step in addressing the problem of ethnic hate crimes begins with the individual and his or her belief system regarding human nature and the capacity of human nature to change and improve based on the context of community interaction.

Growth through Giving

A further aim of this text is in illustrating the concept that the very best that people are capable of providing to each other is through their relationships with each other and contributing to the community itself. Thus, the community and society provides the environment that triggers positive behaviors for each other and not destruction. The community is the foundation within any group and allows people to exchange their skills and potential with each other that ultimately provides a sense of meaning and purpose for all persons residing within that community. When individuals feel as though they have something to offer other community members (regardless of race or ethnicity), there no longer remains a need to engage in conflict, prejudice or antisocial behaviors.

Does prejudice and ethnic conflict exist today? The answer is clearly yes. Can these problems become addressed and can we influence cooperative behaviors among ethnically diverse groups? Absolutely — just as long as people remember that they control their behaviors and that they are provided with opportunities to contribute to the greater good of society.

People can make positive changes in their lives, and often working with the very types of persons that they have had previous conflicts with is the best way to overcome bias and prejudice. We hope that we have provided you with a thorough description of the advantages and necessity of community service work as well as its applications to multiethnic and diverse societies. Not only do we have the capacity to make these positive changes in our lives, but making positive changes will not only improve our life, but the community at large.

Our behaviors, our styles of communication and how we establish relationships with others all stem from decisions and choices that we make. Reducing and ultimately eliminating prejudice and discrimination ultimately is a matter of how we decide to monitor our lives and our choices— things that we maintain control over. Teaching our children to value and respect others requires a commitment that we must adhere to on a daily basis. Teaching respect and communication is an important start in teaching tolerance to all groups. Teaching individuals that they do have control over behaviors and that we are in fact capable of making positive choices and contributions to our society are critical factors necessary in improving the context of our relations with each other.

The three primary characteristics that community service work provides for people in helping diverse groups to better understand each other include:

- Cognitive Revision. Literally defined, cognitive revision mean "rethinking" negative attitudes once held towards other groups. In cognitive revision, older adults can recognize the importance and value of change (something not easily accomplished at the late adulthood stage). Cognitive revision may include changes in attitudes that are counterproductive and negative stereotypes. In many different types of social exchanges and daily interaction, reducing prejudice and discrimination may be as simple as making a cognitive effort to change not only how we think, but what we think. Changing our thoughts relative to how we view other members of different races) can be as simple as "Just say no to racism."
- Interdependence. Recognizing the need to balance independence with interdependence is also vital in late adulthood. Independence in knowing that the older adult can still function autonomously, yet interdependence in knowing that our relationships with others influence how we feel about ourselves. When we engage in community service work with others, we feel happier about ourselves by contributing to the welfare of others. Becoming more involved in community outreach efforts, and collaboration skills all involve one critical and related feature: *Interdependence*. Interdependence refers to the realization that our existence and welfare depend (in part) in the development of our relationship with others. When we feel as though we belong and have achieved a sense of connectedness we are more likely to improve our relationships with others.
- Collaboration. Recognizing our need to share our ideas and views regarding our behaviors with other people is critical in late adulthood. Working with others in cooperative or collaborative groups allows us to exchange our ideas with each other and improve our relationships with each other. When groups of persons exchange ideas and work towards a common goal, their experiences and qualitative relationships improve significantly. Creating more interethnic cooperative task forces in our community, such as improvements in civic activities, cleaning parks, and helping communities address social problems are key methods in reducing ethnocentrism, ethnic conflict, and ethnocentrism.

Appendix A

Understanding Immigration Reform and Ethnocentrism from the Cuban Perspective

BY DR. NORMA ESPINOSA PARKER

Introduction

One of the primary reasons why the authors of this volume have put our thoughts and efforts together in writing a text designed to improve interethnic group relationships was the dramatic increases in hate crimes and the anti-immigration fervor that has been slowly developing among different ethnic groups within the United States. An additional area of concern that is now becoming a very contentious interethnic, cultural and even political issue is that of immigration and border control. As educators and psychologists, we have felt (and continue to feel) that diversity provides both strength and unity among all groups of people and builds a stronger community. We also feel that our strongest weapon in the fight against discrimination and ethnocentrism is through education and understanding the needs and cultural practices of the diverse groups that we share our community with. One of the historical problems that has contributed to the development of ethnocentrism is our failure in understanding the relationship between the needs and cultural practices between the minority group (the out-group) in relation to the dominant group. Collectively, as a society and community that embraces the concepts of diversity, we need to better understand the needs of all groups and communicate with each other how these goals (economic, interpersonal and professional) may be achieved.

Dr. Norma Espinosa Parker is a Cuban immigrant who has achieved the American Dream. Dr. Espinosa Parker has balanced *her traditional Cuban culture and history and has assimilated into the dominant culture without sacrificing her own Cuban identity. Theoretical reviews are interesting relative to controversial topics in academia; however, few individuals can dispute the accuracy of someone who has actually experienced these problems of discrimination relative to ethnicity. Dr. Espinosa Parker has vital information and experiences that we hope you can understand relative to our topics of immigration, ethnic identity and ethnocentrism in modern society.*

In her essay following, Dr. Espinosa Parker describes her unique perspective from both the immigrant (the out-group) as well as the dominant group viewpoints. She is a successful teacher and professor in higher education. Dr. Espinosa Parker has committed herself to improving the quality of living through higher education and currently teaches English as a Second Language.

When we respect others we can celebrate our differences. Cel-

With *UNDERSTANDING* comes

TOLERANCE.* *With tolerance comes

ACCEPTANCE.

With acceptance comes

RESPECT

ebration of our differences helps unites us in a common goal: Understanding "those people" who are so very much like we are. Breaking the stereotypes often requires finding common ground among diverse groups who also share common goals.

What Does Immigration Really Mean?

I was born in Havana, Cuba. I am a third-generation Cuban by birth *and* I am an American by choice. My family and I came to the United States at the height of Castro's regime and at the beginning of a very dark period in the United States—the Civil Rights unrest and hence the movement. These were two very difficult and mind-boggling events that struck a fear in us. We had no problems understanding one of this events—communism took over our country so we no longer had a homeland.

The second event — the Civil Rights unrest and movement — was, and still is, much more difficult to understand. It was difficult because we in Cuba did not know that African Americans had no rights, could not vote and could not live any where near white areas. The Civil Rights movement strove to change these conditions. In many ways it succeeded, but when you look back, the status quo remains.

What We Encountered: Ethnocentricity, Prejudice and Discrimination

As soon as we settled in the United States, my mother sat us down and told us that from that moment forward we were to continue with our education, learn English and behave as if we were still in Cuba, going to school and studying music. My mother wanted to enroll my younger sisters in a good Christian school. Someone recommended the Hawthorne Christian School as an excellent school, so my mother went to that school to start the enrollment process. They took the information and told my mother they would be calling her within two days. My mother waited, and waited and they did not call so my mother decided to call them. They informed her that at the moment they did not have any scholarships available and gave my mother some other reasons that did not make any sense. Soon after, my mother learned that the school was an all-white school and they had no intention in allowing any student of color into their school. My mother started to look for another school, never mentioning to my sisters the reasons why she was looking for another school. Later on she told us that she did not want to poison our minds with the racism and discrimination that prevailed in the United States.

After doing some research into schools suitable for us, in 1962 we were enrolled in the Los Angeles High School English as a Second Language Program. We did not speak any English so we were enrolled in an ESL class. In my class there were twenty-five students learning English and none of us spoke the same language. The students came from Russia, China, Germany, Lithuania, Brazil, France and Cuba. Since my sister was in the class with me, obviously we had to be separated. The teacher, Mrs. Elder, whom I still remember quite fondly, said to the class: "From now on I want each and every one of you to read, speak, write and listen to everything in English. I want you to breathe, eat, sleep in English. Since none of us spoke English she performed some body language, pirouettes, hand and facial motions and other strange motions to make us understand what she meant. Our minds were a very fertile ground for any teacher who was the center of attention. It worked. In three months we were all speaking, reading, and writing English.

Understanding "Those People" Who Are So Very Much Like Us

One of my most indelible experiences, one which is seared in my brain forever, is what I learned from observing students during my first weeks in an American high school. Since Cuba was and is a very diverse society with diverse demographics, the diverse student population in Los Angeles High School was comforting at first. There were students from all over the world. However, there seemed to be invisible lines grouping and keeping people in place according to race and color of skin. White students all grouped together, African Americans did the same, Asian American students also grouped away from the rest while the foreign students just stood by and watched. The unfriendly, puzzling, and confusing invisible line divided them all.

But This Wasn't the Worst Part

Coming from a small country where you really know your neighbors and friendliness, caring for each other and reaching out to each other were our way of life, what happened next was a lifelong learning experience. First, we had been given instructions by our ESL teacher to find students and practice our English skills with them so during recess that's what we set out to do. The first group of students we encountered were Caucasians. A fellow student and I approached them and of course, I, being a woman of color and proud of it, was instantly rejected by the whites. However, as soon as I opened my mouth and started speaking in my very broken English, their attitude changed and they opened up and welcomed me.

The complete opposite happened, however, when we approached the African American students. At first they welcomed us immediately until we tried to communicate. The obvious came through — we were foreigners and, consequently, not one of them. They went as far as to tell us in a disparaging manner that since we were Cubans we were not one of them; we were not black Americans.

That day when we got home we mentioned this phenomenon to our mother. Since she had visited the United States in two previous occasions she understood instantly and asked one question: Are there any students from Latin America and other countries? Of course, yes, we answered, so she simply said make friends with them and stay with them. Then she said something that stuck with me through my growing and development years in the U.S. "Forget about the racist behavior of others. That is their problem, don't make it yours. Always be proud of who you are, respect others and tolerate their idiosyncrasies which come from ignorance. They don't know who you are so they are judging you superficially. What you need to do is focus on learning English and your studies. Remember, you are in a foreign country so learn about its culture, its people and respect others and they will respect you. Don't lose your culture or your beliefs and don't ever forget who you are. Color of skin has never been an issue, it wasn't an issue in Cuba, don't let it become an issue in the United States. You know who, what, and how you are. Be proud of that, your identity was established at birth and it will always be so." This was a very valuable lesson.

Asking the Questions — Difficult or Not

Here are the difficult questions that we all need to ask:

1. What are children learning at home? What do they see? What do they hear?
2. What examples and role models do they have?
3. What are they learning at school?
4. What responsibilities do schools have to children?
5. How do we change the status quo to foster collaboration and growth? Institutions of higher learning must become change agents working cohesively and collaboratively with a shared purpose and common goal.
6. Immigration and its effect on society, educational systems, multiethnic student population, race, prejudice and discrimination and ethnocentrisms?
7. And how do immigration issues affect interpersonal relations?

What Is Happening to the Children?

Fifty, forty, thirty, even twenty-five years ago, children were raised in homes with two parents, sometimes with grandparents, intricate and important members of the family. Family gatherings were the norm instead of the exception. The father was the breadwinner and the mother stayed at home to raise the children. She took care of them; made sure they were fed, clothed and nurtured as well as disciplined when necessary. Children had help with homework and both parents took the time to read to them, take them to the library and the park and did all the things that help children grow into productive citizens.

In contrast, and according to the 2000 U.S. Census, a large number of families are single-parent homes due to divorce, death and, many times, incarceration. This problem is even more prevalent in innercity homes where teenage pregnancy has contributed to this phenomenon.

Most Remain at Home — by Themselves

Clearly, children are left to fend for themselves. There is no adult at home when they get home from school or maybe a sibling, not much older than the child, is home to take care of them or fix them a meal or a snack, but the sibling, must of the time, is in need herself. So the outcome is that homework is left undone and they eat whatever they can get, many times fast food.

What awaits a child at home is the T.V or computer games, if they go home at all. When the parent gets home from a minimum wage job, she/he is too tired to cook, too grumpy to help with homework or answer questions and barely listen to what they have to say about their day. At times violence is the norm. Many times the family is on social welfare to supplement the income and even so, it isn't enough. So the next logical question then is what are children learning at home? Who/what role models do they have?

Children, and adults for that matter, need to interact with others; however, while a child is being shaped and developed, that child will emulate others. It is a proven fact that by the time a child gets to school his/her persona is already shaped. Whatever else enters his/her life from observing and emulating others just adds to ongoing character development. Children need to interact for their sense of being, a sense of who they are and most importantly, for the sense of belonging.

What Happens When Needs Are Not Met at Home?

If children don't have their needs met at home, they will be met somewhere and by somebody else: hence, gangs. In inner cities all over the United States, gangs have taken over neighborhoods, families, children and businesses. These gangs control by violence: you either accept their code of conduct or you don't belong; if you don't belong, you are marked. This is a huge problem and this problem affects everyone; however, people don't get involved because the problem is in "the hood, not in my neighborhood." Children's innocence is being robbed. Living in poverty, without parental support at home, they are wooed into joining gangs because they offer them that support, that sense of belonging they don't receive at home or at school.

On May 31, 2007, *Anderson Cooper 360*, a newsmagazine program, reported and interviewed many young people from a community in Chicago where it was reported that in the first five months of 2007, 28 young people had died from violent acts. The show was called "Twenty-Four Hours in Chicago" and Cooper examined the 5/10/07 death of a sixteen-year old who was shot by another teenager who opened fire on a bus.

The young people interviewed expressed their reality as living in the midst of gangs but did not belong to the gangs. They are working hard in schools, getting jobs, and keeping out of trouble, but that was never reported by the media. In their view, the media only reported all the horrible and negative acts that take place in their neighborhood, but the positive acts were never reported, or the struggles of the good people that live not by choice, but by circumstances beyond their control, which keep them in the "hood." One of the young ladies interviewed stated the fact that the media, movies, and rappers overemphasized murders, drugs and gangs and, in short, paint every person of color with the same brush. She further stated that people watching the news and the movies or listening to the rappers, all they see about them is drugs, gangs and violence, and there was no reaction from the people watching because they don't care. After all, all that violence is in the hood, not in suburbia.

Mayor Daly was also interviewed. His comments were insightful and he asked questions: What is the role of parents in community policing, in their own homes and with their own children? Should they take matters into their own hands and search their children's rooms, school bags, closets, everything? What is the role of the churches? Mayor Daly further stated that "it is not one person, or the police alone, or just the schools; it is the job of the entire community changing one block at a time."

What Are Middle and High School Students Learning in School?

According to the K-12 school districts, students might be engaged in effective learning with the latest technological support (i.e., a computer per student), the best prepared teachers have been hired; resources and community involvement and access to financial support. Preparation for exit exams and SAT tutoring is available, no matter the cost, and students learn. Obviously, the school districts mentioned are not attended by minority students, nor are they racially or culturally diverse students. The students privileged enough to enroll in these schools are white students with the sense of entitlement and the rights which are denied to minority students. Those are the students being prepared for college, for future high-level positions and for leadership. Hence the status quo remains.

It is a proven fact that students in innercity school districts do not have the advantages that the above-mentioned schools have. In many instances, high school students are just taking a place or filling a seat until they graduate. They are in overcrowded classrooms; many experience racial violence for lack of mutual understanding; they are not prepared for exit exams; tutoring is not available and, as mentioned before, the mere fact that many of them speak little or no English or English is their second language labels them as illiterate or as not being intelligent. In many instances, students are not being challenged academically; consequently, upon graduation (if they graduate and don't drop out) they opt to, or are encouraged to, enroll in vocational programs, or have to go to work at some fast food restaurant or factory without a chance for a future. It is clear that schools are not preparing this group of students for the workforce or for higher education. The outcome is that colleges and universities are accepting and enrolling students who are in need of basic and remedial education. For many of these students, who see the possibilities once they are attending these institutions, this is the opportunity of last resort.

Parents who are concerned for their children's education work hard and try to inculcate or impress upon their children the fact that their future is in education. But many things deter them from their goals, or they impress more the need to excel in sports or become an artist so they can make a lot of money.

In my case there was no choice. It did not matter that we were in a different culture, a different country with a different language: education was a must — no ifs or buts about it. It didn't matter how long it'd take, or who was against us, or who discriminated against us, nothing would deter us from our educational goal. Was it easy? On the contrary, it was a constant struggle.

My Struggle to Get an Education

Education is a very important factor for Cubans. Whether in Cuba or in the United States, I knew I would get a college education, and not just an education, but I would strive to achieve the highest possible degree, no matter the cost or how long it'd take. My grandparents, parents, aunts and uncles were educators and musicians and they taught piano, organ, voice and choir. So, as you can see, education was a given. I attended the Conservatory of Music from the time I was seven years old until we left Cuba. At times, like any other child, I would try to rebel from having so much homework, so much practice, so much studying to do, but it didn't do any good. My mother taught all six sisters to sing together so I didn't see why we had to learn to play the piano and guitar as well as sing, but we just had to do it. My mother also wanted us to learn English, but after complaining a lot and reminding her how much we already had to do, and besides we spoke Spanish in Cuba, so we didn't need to learn English. We won and she relented, but not before telling us that someday we would regret it.

Then on our first day of school in America, we came home with homework and asked my mother for help with the vocabulary, she could not help but remind us of the fact that she wanted us to learn English while we were in Cuba. Now we needed if and we were going to have to do it pretty much on our own.

The first five years in the United States were difficult. We could not work because we were waiting for our legal papers and were going to school. Some people who saw our struggle suggested to my mother that she could get government assistance for us while we got on our feet. My mother told them thank you but no thanks. We had never been on government assistance in Cuba and under no circumstance were we going to be on government assistance in the United States. So we supported ourselves by singing every weekend. We sang in 2 to 3 churches every weekend. When the school year ended we embarked on a singing tour of the United States, Canada and Mexico. We sang in churches and auditoriums, the New York World's Fair and the Seattle World's Fair. We returned home two days before the beginning of school so that we could enroll and attend our classes. That's how we supported ourselves the first five years.

Upon graduation from high school I started to work full time and attended college full time as well. The goal, again, was education. It took me a bit longer to finish college but I graduated with a BA with honors. I got married and had my daughter but continued with my educational goals. I received a MA in Education with an emphasis in Spanish and Bilingual Education. This was difficult and demanding because I was working full time and had more responsibilities. At times I wanted to give up, especially when I was diagnosed with lupus, but I struggled through and finished the MA. I continued to work full time but took a break from studying. I became a full-time instructor teaching ESL and Spanish, but my goal of a higher education degree never left me. Circumstances, health issues and finance prevented me from pursuing that goal. Ten years later I had the opportunity to pursue my goal and I enrolled in the Doctoral/PhD program at Nova Southeastern University. My goal was to finish the program in five years; health issues took their toil on me. It took me longer than I wanted but I finished it and completed the goal I had set for myself.

What Is the Role of the School, Teachers, Instructors, Counselors, and Professors in the Effort to Bring about Change?

Our role as teachers, instructors, professors, counselors, community leaders and parents must be to foster and foment change that will teach students the importance of collaboration, working together towards a common goal, healthy competition, and promoting the "we" instead of the "I."

We must become agents of change and mentors as well as examples to those who are observing everything we do and listening to what we say. As leaders, we must change, and change takes time and preparation. In creating any kind of change, the hardest factor is making the case for change and convincing people that change is needed. Change should be a natural part of life; however, it is a very difficult process to accomplish.

We, as leaders, must celebrate our students' diversity, culture, languages, talents, and abilities. Some schools celebrate special days that represent the cultural background of a group of students; parents, students, and the community become involved. However, attention must be given to making sure that the special celebrations are not just for the group celebrating its own day as cultural pride. These events and celebrations should be viewed as an avenue of introduction to other groups who have different cultural backgrounds. In this manner the process for mutual understanding is started, which in turns will lead to communication between culturally diverse groups. Mentors and counselors play an extremely important role in this area, as well as in helping resolve conflicts.

Collaboration between Groups

As a language professor, I teach English as a Second Language and Spanish. The college where I teach is located in southern California, where the demographic has undergone extreme changes in the last thirty years.

This change in turn has transferred to universities and institutions in the area, but especially in our college. The college demographics has change from mostly whites and Jewish in the 1960s to 49 percent Hispanic, 51 percent African American, 2 percent whites and 4 percent Asian American and Native American. This demographic is represented in my classes as well. In my Spanish classes I have 90 percent African Americans who are trying to learn to communicate in Spanish and 10 percent of the students are of Hispanic descent, born in the United States, also trying to improve their written and conversational Spanish. Obviously, the ESL classes are comprised of Hispanic students (of which 85 percent are from Mexico). The tension between the two groups is palpable.

As a Cuban and a woman of color, this is an intolerable situation and a recipe for fomenting division, discrimination and misunderstandings. In an effort to foster communication first of the learning process and second of understanding "those people" who are so similar to ourselves, in collaboration with my colleagues, a process has been implemented for communication, in which students from ESL classes and students from Spanish classes are encouraged to communicate with each other in both English and Spanish. In this process ESL classes are assigned group interviews with the Spanish classes. Students must use what they have learned in their classes and formulate questionnaires in the targeted language.

During the semester, classes will take turns visiting each other's classroom. A student learning English will be paired with a student learning Spanish; obviously, they are from different cultures and race. For five minutes each student has the opportunity to interview the other in his/her second language and listen to answers given in that language. After five minutes the second student interviews the other student in his/her second language and will listen to responses in that language. Students must help each other with language pronunciation and spelling. During the one-hour-long class, each student must interview as many students as possible. Upon returning to their own classrooms each student must give an oral presentation in the target language. They must give information to the rest of the class as to whom they met, where they were from, where they live, if they have brothers and sisters, and any other information they were able to elicit. This process is done three to four times a semester and as many as six classes are involved.

This process has proven to be very effective in helping students with their second language acquisition and has opened communications with each other on a daily basis. This process is also helping students understand each other's differences as well as appreciate each others similarities by communicating in the two languages.

Education and Demographics
as a Societal Factor

The U.S. Census 1960–1990 demonstrates that the Hispanic population is the fastest growing group in the United States. This group is very heterogeneous, composed of individuals from many countries with varying degrees of acculturation, income, and citizenship status. This group grew from 5 percent in 1960 to 10 percent in 1995. There has been a 50 percent increase from 15 million in 1980 to 22.5 million in the 1990 (Bureau of Census of 1980 and 1990). The U.S. Census of 2000 demonstrates that the Hispanic population has nearly doubled since the last census (a large percentage of those are here under illegal status). According to Carrasquillo & Rodriguez, this group has the same need as the other immigrant groups: the need to learn English.

In *The New Demographics*, Treadwell painted a bleak picture in his prediction of the future demographics for the 0 to seventeen-year-old population. His prediction has already taken place. For instance, he states that the Hispanic population will have grown from 6 million to 19 million by the year 2020; the black population will have increased by 22 percent, to 12 million, while the white population will have decreased by 6 million. It is obvious that the Hispanic population is the fastest growing, of which 63 percent are of Mexican descent.

This migration brings to schools children with no English skills. Garcia (1993) states that these students:

1. Are characterized by substantive participation in a non–English-speaking social environment.
2. Have acquired the normal communicative abilities of that social environment.
3. Are exposed to a substantive English environment, more than likely for the first time, during the formal schooling process.

Statistics show that of this group 50 percent have no high school diploma; California, Texas and New York are home to 65 percent of the Hispanic population in the United States; twenty-two percent fall below the poverty level compared with nine percent of non–Hispanic families.

Effects of Immigration
on the Educational System

Demographics changes in the United States have brought minority and ethnic issues related to language and education to the forefront of discussions. It is obvious, now more than ever, that the gap between the majority and the minority groups have increased and will continue to increase unless schools, training institutions, colleges and universities start to provide skill-building classes for students in the process of learning English. The gap between the haves and have-nots continues to get wider and wider, making the issue educational as well as economical.

According to Peter Sacks (2007), the educational system has had to change in order to provide, at least on the surface, more equality in education for minority and limited-English-speaking students. These changes brought about affirmative action, which in turn created a lot of controversy in higher education. Affirmative action attempted to bridge the educational equality gap between whites and minorities. He further states, "significant changes in the landscape of educational opportunity over the past thirty years have been the democratization of a 'college-going culture' for previously underrepresented group...." However, he brings up the point that in terms of who expected to go to college and who actually applied to college, the differences between whites and most minorities declined to negligible quantities. The question that we as a collective society now need to ask of ourselves is *why*?

Appendix B

Directly from the People

HOW COMMUNITY SERVICE
WORK HAS CHANGED THE
LIVES OF INDIVIDUALS
WITHIN THE COMMUNITY

One way to illustrate to the reader the effectiveness of community service work is in highlighting some of the experiences of the actual students who were involved in the work itself. Some of the most memorable and touching experiences in community service work is in seeing how relationships between individuals who recently were strangers have transformed and developed into a strong bond of trust and friendship. Some of these comments are very personal, and we include them here to provide a deep and personal insight to the positive psychological effects of community service work:

- "It was amazing that I was experiencing the same sense of pride and gratification of putting in so much effort in a short amount of time and seeing the results.... [T]here was a feeling of elation simply because I knew volunteering with other people from different backgrounds and schools was such a positive experience for everyone. The day actually felt like it went by in 2 hours, not 5 hours." (Cammy M.)
- "As I was planting the flowers, I was thinking about how gardening was really calming and helping me to relax.... Taking out my frustration with a shovel, pulling out irritating weeds, and planting beautiful flowers felt great.... As we finished our endeavor, I really felt proud of our accomplishment. It was like finishing an art piece. Gardening has the same sort of rush especially since the area that we were working on looked horrible, and to the differences from our work really made it worthwhile." (Theresa N.)

201

- "I really enjoyed the gardening experience a lot more than I actually thought I would.... I've never really been one to enjoy outdoor activities like gardening but I really feel like I got a lot out this experience. After we finished the areas assigned to us, I felt a strong sense of accomplishment, even though I was only digging [cultivating] in the dirt. It definitely was a lot harder than I thought it was to cultivate soil. Nevertheless, it felt great to contribute to such a beautiful thing like this garden." (Anna S.)
- "I started off cultivating and weeding the walkway and started to work with three other volunteers.... [W]e easily started up a conversation and I soon learned that one woman who was working next to me wanted to become a pediatric nurse. I told her that I was in school at Pepperdine for psychology and that my career path was undecided, but that I was enjoying the ride and anxious to graduate. We causally continued our conversation while working in the grade for a few more minutes before she got up and watered the plants. Conversing with her and working in the garden were two of the activities I enjoyed the most. I noticed that the people working in the garden were from every walk of life and they took pride in maintaining and caring for the garden." (Jaclynn R.)
- "My overall experiences in the community gardening program were more positive than I had anticipated. I was surprised to see a broad range of different individuals from various economic classes and ethnic backgrounds. The work definitely provided me with the opportunity to talk and begin to bond with the people who were working in close proximity to me. My stereotypes were (unsurprisingly) totally wrong. I wish that I had more Saturday mornings available this semester because I definitely would have benefited myself from further visits, and I think that I too could have been a good mentor for the students. I wish to commend the Northridge mentors for doing a very good job in organizing the project. And not incidentally, the garden was *beautiful*." (Cynthia G.)
- "Gardening is something that I have never done before, not even at my own home. So for me to get up early on a Saturday morning and help was a big commitment. It was a pleasant experience for me and I can honestly say that the work was tiring but rewarding. The project helped me to understand how pleasurable it is in giving back to a community and work with others towards a common goal." (Azad G.)
- "Where I go to school we really do not have much of an opportunity to meet different people from different backgrounds and experiences. While working in the Compton community service program I was able

to meet many people and get an idea about who they were through the gardening program. I would do it again in a minute because it helped me to understand people from different backgrounds—something that is very important in my clinical work." (Nick P.)

Bibliography

Adler, A. (1929). *The practice and theory of individual psychology*. New York: Harcourt, Brace & World.

_____. (1927). *Understanding human nature*. New York: Garden City Publishing Company, Inc.

Aronson, E. (1986, August). *Teaching students things they think they already know all about: The case of prejudice and desegregation*. Paper presented at the meeting of the American Psychology Association, Washington, D.C.

Au, T. K., Knightly, L. M., Jun, S-A., & Oh, J. S. (2002). Overhearing a language during childhood. *Psychological Science, 13*, 238–242.

Bandura, A., Ross, D., & Ross, S. (1963). Imitation of film-mediated aggressive models. *Journal of Abnormal and Social Psychology, 66*, 3–11.

_____. (1969). *Principles of behavior modification*. New York: Holt, Rinehart and Winston.

Baumrind, D. (1991). Effective parenting during the adolescent transition. In R. M. Learner, A. C. Peterson, & J. Brooks-Gunn (Eds.), *Family transitions*, Hillsdale, N.J.: Erlbaum.

Bavelier, D., Newport, E. L., & Supalla, T. (2003). Children need natural languages, signed or spoken. *Cerebrum, 5(1)*, 19–32.

Beck, A. T. (1993). Cognitive therapy: Past, present and future. *Journal of Consulting and Clinical Psychology, 61*, 194–198.

Bennett, M., Barrett, M., Karakozov, R., Kipiani, G., Lyons, E., Pavlenko, V., & Riazanova, T. (2004). Young children's evaluations of the ingroup and of outgroups: A multi-national study. *Social Development, 13(1)*, 124–141.

Biccchieri, C. & Green M. (1997). Symmetry arguments for cooperation in the Prisoner's Dilemma. In Holmstro_m-Hintikka, G., & Tuomela, R. (1997). *Contemporary action theory*. Synthese library, v. 266–267. Dordrecht: Kluwer Academic.

Brace, J. J., Morton, J. B., & Munakata, Y. (2006). When actions speak louder than words: Improving children's flexibility in a card-sorting task. *Psychological Science, 17(8)*, 665–669.

Branscombe, N. R., Doosje, B., & McGarty, C. (2002). Antecedents and consequences of collective guilt. In D. M. Mackie & E. R. Smith (Eds.), *From prejudice to intergroup emotions: Differentiated reactions to social groups* (pp. 49–66). Philadelphia: Psychology Press.

Brewer, M. B., & Brown, R. J. (1998). Intergroup relations. In D. T. Gilbert, S. T. Fiske, et al. (Eds.), *The handbook of social psychology* (Vol. 2, 4th ed.) (pp. 554–594). Boston: McGraw-Hill.

Brewer, M. B., & Gaertner, S. L., (2001). Toward a reduction of prejudice: Intergroup contact and social categorization. In R. Brown & S. L. Gaertner (Eds.), *Handbook of social psychology: Intergroup processes*. Maiden, M.A.: Blackwell.

Brislin, R. (1993). *Understanding culture's influence on behavior*. Fort Worth, T.X.: Harcourt Brace.

Bruno, J. E. (1997). *It's About Time: Leading School Reform in an Era of Time Scarcity*. Thousand Oaks, C.A.: Corwin Press, Inc.

Burnstein, E., Crandall, C., & Kitayama, S. (1994). Some neo-Darwinian decision rules for altruism: Weighing cues for inclusive fitness as a function of the biological importance of the decision. *Journal of Personality & Social Psychology, 67*, 773–789.

Buss, D. M. (1999). *Evolutionary psychology: The new science of the mind*. Boston: Allyn and Bacon.

_____. (2000). Evolutionary psychology. In A. Kazdin (Ed.), *Encyclopedia of psychology*. Washington, D.C., & New York: American Psychology and Oxford University Press.

Chambers, J. R., Baron, R. S., & Inman, M. L. (2006). Misperceptions in intergroup conflict: Disagreeing about what we disagree about. *Psychological Science, 17*, 38–45.

Conyers, J. E. (2002). Racial inequality: Emphasis on explanations. *Western Journal of Black Studies, 26*(4), 249–254.

Darwin, C. (1859). *The origin of the species*. New York: Gramercy Books.

Davis, M. H., Luce, C. & Kraus, S. J. (1994). The heritability of characteristics associated with dispositional empathy. *Journal of Personality, 62*, 369–391.

Dovidio, J. F., Gaertner, S. L., & Validzic, A. (1998). Intergroup bias: Status differentiation and a common ingroup identity. *Journal of Personality and Social Psychology, 75*, 109–120.

Dunn, J. (1992). Siblings and development. *Current Directions in Psychological Science, 1*, 6–11.

Erikson, E. (1963). *Childhood and society*. New York: Norton.

Faludi, S. (1992). *Backlash: The undeclared war against American women*. New York: Doubleday.

Feagin, J. R., & McKinney, K. D. (2003). *The many costs of racism*. Lanham, M.D.: Rowman & Littlefield.

Ferber, J. (2007). Encouraging a culture of interest in others: American and Russian children connect. *Community Works Journal*, 13–16.

Gould, S. J. (1996, September). The diet of worms and the defenestration of Prague. *Natural History*, 18–24, 64, 66–67.

Graham, S., Weiner, B., & Zucker, G. S. (1997). An attributional analysis of punishment goals and public reactions to O. J. Simpson. *Personality and Social Psychology Bulletin, 23*, 331–346.

Heine, S. J., & Norenzayan, A. (2006). Toward a psychological science for a cultural species. *Perspectives on Psychological Science, 3*, 251–269.

Henline, B. H. (2006). *Technology use and intimacy development in committed relationships: Exploring the influence of differentiation of self*. Unpublished dissertation, Texas Tech University.

Hess, E., & Petrovich, S. (1977). *Imprinting*. Dowden, Hutchinson and Ross Publishers, Inc.

Hill, R. (2003). The role of racial dialogue in education: Preparation for living in a multiracial society. *The Journal of Negro Education, 72*(2), 208–216.

Hodson, G., & Sorrentino, R. M. (2001). Just who favors in in-group? Personality differences in reactions to uncertainty in the minimal group paradigm. *Group Dynamics, 5,* 92–101.

Hoffman, A. J. (1995). Collaborative group work as effective measures in reducing ethnocentrism and increasing prosocial behaviors among community college students. *Dissertation Abstracts International* (University Microfilms No. 9523606).

_____, & Wallach, J. N. (2006). Improving interpersonal communication through community service work and a gardening project: Leave the cell phones at home. *The Community College Enterprise.*

_____, and _____. (2007). Reducing self-entitlement through community service participation. *The Community College Journal, 13,* 81–82.

Hovland, C. I., & Sears, R. R. (1940). Minor studies in aggression: VI. Correlation of lynchings with economic indices. *Journal of Psychology, 9,* 301–310.

Iard, C. (1991). *The psychology of emotions.* New York: Plenum.

Jellison, J. M., & Green, J. (1981). A self-presentation approach to the fundamental attribution error: The norm of internality. *Journal of Personality and Social Psychology, 40,* 643–649.

Johnson, C. L., & Troll, L. (1994). Constraints and facilitators to friendship in late adult life. *The Gerontologist, 34,* 79–87.

Johnson, D. W., & Johnson, F. (2003). *Joining together: Group theory and group skills.* (8th ed.). Boston: Allyn & Bacon.

Kardong, K. (2008). *Introduction to biological evolution* (2nd ed.). New York: McGraw-Hill.

Kawakami, K., Dovidio, J. F., Moll, J., Hermsen, S., & Russn, A. (2000). Just say no (to stereotyping): Effects of training in the negation of stereotypic associations on stereotype activation. *Journal of Personality and Social Psychology, 24,* 407–416.

Kazdin, A. E. (2003). Problem-solving skills training and parent management for conduct disorder. In A. E. Kazdin & J. R. Weisz (Eds.), *Evidence-based psychotherapies for children and adolescents* (pp. 241–262). New York: Guilford Press.

Kitzmann, K. M., Cohen, R., & Lockwood, R. L. (2002). Are only children missing out? Comparison of the peer-related social competence of only children and siblings. *Journal of Social and Personal Relationships, 19,* 299–316.

Lambert, A. J. (1995). Stereotypes and social judgment: The consequences of group variability. *Journal of Personality and Social Psychology, 68,* 388–403.

Leung, A. K., Maddux, W. M., Galinsky, A. D., & Chiu, C. (2008). Multicultural experience enhances creativity. *American Psychologist, 63,* 169–181.

Lewin, K. (1951). *Field theory in social science.* New York: Harper.

Ma, H. K., Shek, D. T. L., Cheung, P. C., & Tam, K. K. (2002). A longitudinal study of peer and teacher influences on prosocial and antisocial behavior of Hong Kong Chinese adolescents. *Social Behavior and Personality, 30,* 157–168.

Maslow, A. (1968). *Toward a psychology of being* (2nd ed.). Princeton, N.J.: Van Nostrand.

Mayer, J. D., & Hanson, E. (1995). Mood-congruent judgment over time. *Personality and Social Psychology Bulletin, 21,* 237–244.

Morris, M. W., & Pang, K. (1994). Culture and cause: American and Chinese attributions for social and physical events. *Journal of Personality and Social Psychology, 67,* 949–971.

Moscovici, S. (1985). Social influence and conformity. In G. Lindzey & E. Aronson (Eds.), *Handbook of social psychology* (3rd. ed.), New York: Random House.

Oakes, P. J., Haslam, S. A., & Turner, J. C. (1994). *Stereotyping and social reality.* Oxford: Blackwell.

Ohman, A., Lundqvist, D., & Esteves, F. (2001). The face in the crowd revisited: Threat advantage with schematic stimuli. *Journal of Personality and Social Psychology, 80,* 381–396

Paolini, S., Hewstone, M., Carins, E., & Voci, A. (2004). Effects of direct and indirect cross-group friendships on judgments of Catholics and Protestants in Northern Ireland: The mediating role of an anxiety-reduction mechanism. *Personality and Social Psychology Bulletin, 30,* 770–786.

Pettgrew, T. F. (1979). The ultimate attribution error: Extending Allport's cognitive analysis of prejudice. *Personality and Social Psychology Bulletin, 5,* 461–476.

_____, & Tropp, L. R. (2006). A meta-analytic test of intergroup contact theory. *Journal of Personality and Social Psychology, 90,* 751–783.

Rogers, C. (1959). A theory of therapy, personality, and interpersonal relationships, as developed in the client-centered framework. In S. Koch (Ed.), *Psychology: A study of a science* (Vol. 3). New York: McGraw-Hill.

Rosenthal, R., & Jacobson, L. (1968). *Pygmalion in the classroom: Teacher expectation and student intellectual development.* New York: Hold, Rinehart, & Winston.

Rushton, J. P., Russell, R. J. H., & Wells, P. A. (1984). Genetic similarity theory: Beyond kin selection. *Behavioral and Brain Sciences, 12,* 503–559.

Sherif, M. (1966). *In common predicament: Social psychology of intergroup conflict and cooperation.* Boston: Houghton Mifflin.

_____, Harvey, D. J., White, B. J., Hood, W. R., & Sherif, C. W. (1961). *The robber's cave experiment.* Norman, O.K.: Institute of Group Relations.

Slavin, R. (1989). Cooperative learning and student achievement. In R. Slavin (Ed.), *School and classroom organization.* Mahwah, N.J.: Erlbaum.

Smith, G., Spillane, N., & Annus, A. (2006). Implications of an emerging integration of universal and culturally specific psychologies. *Perspectives on Psychological Science, 1(3),* 211–233.

Steele, C.M. & Aronson, J. (1995). Stereotype threat and the intellectual test performance of African Americans. *Journal of Applied Developmental Psychology, 27,* 486–493.

Stephen, W. G. (1987). The contact hypothesis in intergroup relations. In C. Hendrick (Ed.), *Group processes and intergroup relations. Review of personality and social psychology* (Vol. 9, pp. 13–40). Beverly Hills, C.A.: Sage.

Tajfel, H. (1982). Social identity and intergroup relations. Cambridge, England: Cambridge University Press.

_____. (1981). Social stereotypes and social groups. In J. C. Turner & H. Giles (Eds.), *Intergroup behavior* (pp. 144–167). Chicago, I.L.: University of Chicago Press.

Triandis, H. C. (1990). Cross-cultural studies of individualism and collectivism. *Nebraska Symposium on Motivation, 1989, 39,* 41–133.

Trivers, R. (1971). The evolution of reciprocal altruism. *The Quarterly Review of Biology, 46,* pp. 35–57.

Tuckman, B. (1965). Developmental sequences in small groups. *Psychological Bulletin, 63,* 384–399.

Turner, J. C. (1991). *Social Influence.* Pacific Grove, CA: Brooks / Cole.

Tykocinski, O. E. (2001). I never had a chance: Using hindsight tactics to mitigate disappointments. *Personality and Social Psychology Bulletin, 27,* 376–382.

Weiner, B. (1985). An attributional theory of achievement motivation and emotion. *Psychological Review, 92,* 548–573.

Wright, S. C., Aron, A., McLaughlin-Volpe, T., & Ropp, S. A. (1997). The extended contact effect: Knowledge of cross-group friendships and prejudice. *Journal of Personality and Social Psychology, 73,* 73–90.

Zajonc, R. B. (1968). Attitudinal effects of mere exposure [monograph]. *Journal of Personality and Social Psychology, 9,* 1–27.

_____. (2001). Mere exposure: A gateway to the subliminal. *Current Directions in Psychological Science, 10,* 224–228.

Index